Living in America
TEACHER RESOURCE SERIES

Knowing Your Rights
and Responsibilities

New Readers Press

Developed originally by BOCES Geneseo Migrant Center with funding from
a U.S. Education Department Office of Vocational and Adult Education,
English Literacy and Civics Education Demonstration Grant

BOCES Geneseo Migrant Center Project Developers:
Curriculum Developers:
  Karen Yamamoto
  Jane Hogan, EdD
Contributors:
  Patricia Edwards
  Timothy J. Sparling
Graphic Designer:
  Eva McKendry

Special thanks to
  Robert E. Lynch, Director, BOCES Geneseo Migrant Center

Living in America Teacher Resource Series: Knowing Your Rights and Responsibilities
ISBN 978-1-56420-531-5

Copyright © 2007 New Readers Press
New Readers Press
A Publishing Division of ProLiteracy
1320 Jamesville Avenue, Syracuse, New York 13210
www.newreaderspress.com

Printed in the United States of America
9 8 7 6 5 4 3

All proceeds from the sale of New Readers Press materials
support literacy programs in the United States and worldwide.

Developmental Editor: Paula Schlusberg
Design and Production Manager: Andrea Woodbury
Illustrations: James Wallace, Linda Tiff
Production Specialist: Jeffrey R. Smith
Cover Design: Andrea Woodbury

Contents

Introduction to the *Living in America* Curriculum..............................7

    Approach to Language Learning 8

    The Curriculum..8

        Curriculum Features 9

        Lesson Features 9

        Lesson Components 10

        Lesson Support Materials....................................10

    Selected Teaching Techniques.......................................12

    Preparation for Using *Living in America* 13

    The *Living in America* Curriculum 14

Unit 1 Getting a Lawyer...15

    Lesson A - Life Skill: Finding Legal Services 16

        Objective, Materials Included, Materials Needed......16

        Central Theme Picture 17

        Oral Language Activity 1 17

        Oral Language Activity 2 18

        Oral Language Activity 3 20

        Oral Language Activity 4 22

        Reading Activity 23

        Writing Activity 25

    Lesson B - Civic Responsibility: Right to an Attorney 26

        Objective, Materials Included, Materials Needed......26

        Civics Introduction: Right to an Attorney 27

        Oral Language Activity 1 28

        Oral Language Activity 2 29

        Oral Language Activity 3 31

        Oral Language Activity 4 32

        Reading Activity 33

Writing Activity 34

Unit Review Activity 36

Photocopy Masters 37

Unit 2 Communicating with Neighbors and the Police.....................59

Lesson A - Life Skill: Social Skills...60

Objective, Materials Included, Materials Needed......................60

Central Theme Picture 61

Oral Language Activity 1 61

Oral Language Activity 2 63

Oral Language Activity 3 65

Oral Language Activity 4 67

Reading Activity 68

Writing Activity 69

Lesson B - Civic Responsibility: Law Enforcement 71

Objectives, Materials Included, Materials Needed 71

Civics Introduction: Law Enforcement 72

Oral Language Activity 1 74

Oral Language Activity 2 75

Oral Language Activity 3 77

Oral Language Activity 4 78

Reading Activity 79

Writing Activity 80

Unit Review Activity 82

Photocopy Masters 83

Unit 3 Understanding Community Responsibilities 112

Lesson A - Life Skill: Your Responsibilities.................................113

Objective, Materials Included, Materials Needed.....................113

Central Theme Picture 114

Oral Language Activity 1 114

Oral Language Activity 2 115

Oral Language Activity 3 117

Oral Language Activity 4 118

Reading Activity 120

Writing Activity 121

Lesson B - Civic Responsibility: Your Rights If Arrested 123

    Objective, Materials Included, Materials Needed 123

    Civics Introduction: Your Rights If Arrested 124

    Oral Language Activity 1 125

    Oral Language Activity 2 126

    Oral Language Activity 3 127

    Oral Language Activity 4 128

    Reading Activity 130

    Writing Activity 131

Unit Review Activity 133

Photocopy Masters 134

Unit 4 Understanding a Lease 153

Lesson A - Life Skill: How to Rent 154

    Objectives, Materials Included, Materials Needed 154

    Central Theme Picture 155

    Oral Language Activity 1 155

    Oral Language Activity 2 157

    Oral Language Activity 3 159

    Oral Language Activity 4 161

    Reading Activity 162

    Writing Activity 163

Lesson B - Civic Responsibility: Renters' Rights 165

    Objective, Materials Included, Materials Needed 165

    Civics Introduction: Renters' Rights 166

    Oral Language Activity 1 167

    Oral Language Activity 2 168

    Oral Language Activity 3 170

    Oral Language Activity 4 171

    Reading Activity 173

    Writing Activity 174

Unit Review Activity 175

Photocopy Masters 176

Unit 5 Maintaining Housing 193

Lesson A - Life Skill: Home Maintenance 194

    Objective, Materials Included, Materials Needed 194

Central Theme Picture 195
Oral Language Activity 1 195
Oral Language Activity 2 197
Oral Language Activity 3 199
Oral Language Activity 4 201
Reading Activity 202
Writing Activity 203
Lesson B - Civic Responsibility: Renters' Responsibilities 205
Objective, Materials Included, Materials Needed 205
Civics Introduction: Renters' Responsibilities 206
Storyboard 207
Oral Language Activity 1 207
Oral Language Activity 2 210
Oral Language Activity 3 211
Oral Language Activity 4 214
Reading Activity 216
Writing Activity 217
Unit Review Activity 219
Photocopy Masters 220

Generic OK/Not OK Photocopy Master 250

Introduction to the *Living in America* Curriculum

Welcome to *Living in America,* a curriculum tailored to the needs, interests, and language proficiency of literacy-level adult English Language Learners (ELLs). Originally developed primarily for migrant farmworkers, the curriculum is now designed to address the needs of any ELL with very limited literacy and oral skills. **Effectiveness, efficiency,** and **relevance** are the hallmarks of the curriculum. *Living in America* provides a framework for successful learning, with concise, easy-to-follow directions and a selection of topics relevant to the situations and tasks that adult ELLs confront. The development of the curriculum was grounded in a series of learner-centered questions:

- What situations create problems for non-English-speaking adults?
- What life skills would make living in the U.S. easier for non-English-speaking adults?
- What vocabulary and conversation patterns would help facilitate daily communication?
- What civics information regarding legal issues would be pertinent to adult ELLs?
- What knowledge of rights and responsibilities would support community membership?

The design, materials, and strategies selected for the curriculum were guided by a set of instructor-centered questions:

- What lesson design and accompanying materials would best support instructors using the curriculum?
- What teaching strategies would be applicable to a variety of learners and suitable for the variety of instructional settings where those learners are taught?

The resulting curriculum, *Living in America,* provides literacy learners with functional, everyday language that is essential for successfully navigating a new community. Civics-based lessons paired with life-skill lessons help learners understand basic principles, customs, behaviors, and laws in the U.S. The combination of these lessons gives adult learners a voice and access to their rights and responsibilities as contributing community members.

The term "social civics" can be used for norms of expected behavior in situations where a behavior is inappropriate but not illegal. Behaviors and situations stressed in the curriculum are those which may be different from the norms and values in adult

learners' native countries. Carefully selected vocabulary, statements, questions, and related dialogues develop learners' situational language skills, while the civics content fosters understanding and behaviors leading to improved community involvement and acceptance.

The most important force in motivating learners is the instructor's enthusiasm and investment in the curriculum. In *Living in America*, the instructor is the educational decision-maker. Decisions to modify, to reinforce, or to provide more practice are left for the instructor to make.

Approach to Language Learning

The *Living in America* curriculum incorporates an eclectic approach:

- **Communicative Language Instruction** emphasizes the language needed to communicate effectively

- **Total Physical Response** uses nonverbal means of communicating

- **Audio-lingual Instruction** provides the foundation for instructor-directed strategies to teach needed vocabulary and simple sentence patterns within exercises and dialogues

The curriculum focuses on oral competency and comprehension skills, so that learners are able to make their needs known and to understand the information given in response to their questions. Grammar is modeled in the curriculum but not explicitly explained. The curriculum takes the position that if a beginning speaker is understood, sentence form is not as important as the meaning conveyed. Integrating other ESL materials with the *Living in America* curriculum is encouraged and expected, especially to build prerequisite knowledge, including everyday vocabulary as well as letters, colors, dates, numbers, and times.

The Curriculum

Living in America consists of six teacher's resource guides (TRGs). Each TRG presents four to six units on thematically grouped topics. A list of the TRGs and the units in each is found at the end of this Introduction (p. 14). A unit contains two lessons, each designed to be approximately 120 to 180 minutes in length. The four to six instructional hours can be divided flexibly to meet learners' needs and the demands of the instructional setting.

Curriculum Features

Research-Based Strategies

- Model everything first
- Use gestures and body language
- Use realia or authentic materials
- Proceed in a clear instructional sequence: Oral Language → Reading → Writing
- Use a limited number of vocabulary words
- Use and practice vocabulary throughout the lesson
- Proceed from Instructor Model → Group Practice → Individual Practice
- Build on prior knowledge
- Give genuine, positive feedback
- Promote a learning environment that is cooperative, not competitive
- Use constant and consistent repetition and review
- Maintain high, yet reasonable expectations
- Focus on oral understanding and production of English

The curriculum embodies the following:

- **Life skills are paired with civics skills** for successful adjustment to living in and navigating the communities of the U.S.

- **Specific topics are nonsequential,** so that learners' needs and interests can guide topic selection

- **Lessons are adaptable** to any formal or informal learning environment and may be used with groups of various sizes

- **Listening and speaking are emphasized** to meet the needs of beginning learners, who may not be literate in their native languages

- **Research-based teaching strategies are woven** into all lesson activities and learner exercises (see sidebar)

- **A variety of learning styles is supported,** through cues supporting the needs of both visual and auditory learners, and through application activities supporting kinesthetic (hands-on) learners

- **Graphics, vocabulary cards, interactive activities, and activity sheets are included** to facilitate lesson planning and teaching

- **A civics introduction gives background information** about the legal principle supporting each civics lesson

Lesson Features

The lessons are designed to set learners up for success. Because of this, it is desirable to conduct lessons in English. Gestures, mime, drawings, and realia can be used to clarify and enhance understanding and learning. It is best to limit word-for-word translation from the learners' first language. Abstract concepts are an exception, since they are often difficult to comprehend without the support of a first language.

Each lesson includes:

- **Core vocabulary,** illustrated whenever possible and presented on cards

- **Scripted models** of dialogue patterns

- **Suggestions for support gestures and teacher remarks** for eliciting responses and giving praise

- **Model scripts** of oral lesson interactions, where I = Instructor, G = Group, and L = Learner

- **A patterned progression of activities** and repeated activity types to provide consistency for the learners and ease of delivery for the instructor

Lesson Components

Oral Language Activities: Both life-skill and civic-responsibility lessons contain four oral language activities. These begin with interactive vocabulary development, including opportunities for multiple repetition of each target word or phrase. Vocabulary is introduced in a consistent manner for each oral language activity.

Practice Exercises: In each oral language activity, there are practice exercises that incorporate review, enrichment, and application. These practice exercises either allow for cooperative learning or may involve concept development. All exercises model an example of teacher-student interaction and provide step-by-step instructions for easy reference.

Dialogues: Dialogues relate to the theme picture, storyboard, or lesson content. They model a simple conversation appropriate to the context of that lesson. Vocabulary and sentence patterns taught in the lesson are used in the dialogue, providing an opportunity for learners to practice short, focused conversations.

Comprehension Checks: The comprehension check at the end of an activity is a simple and efficient means of assessing whether the material and concepts have been learned. The checks are meant to be done quickly in order to establish whether there is a need for additional practice or whether the group should move forward in the lesson.

Skill Enhancements: Each lesson includes optional reading and writing activities. In reading activities, learners practice recognizing written forms of words or phrases within the context of the lesson. Whenever appropriate, writing activities provide an authentic task, so learners can practice writing something they can use later, like a list of emergency telephone numbers or a repair checklist.

Lesson Support Materials

Each *Living in America* TRG includes photocopy masters (PCMs) of graphics, vocabulary cards, interactive activities, and activity sheets needed to plan and teach lessons. A generic PCM with **OK/Not OK** cards is at the end of the book. In the units, each lesson includes a

Lesson A: Life Skill

- the central theme picture
- four oral language activities
- comprehension checks
- a reading activity
- a writing activity

Lesson B: Civic Responsibility

- a civics introduction
- a storyboard (as appropriate)
- four oral language activities
- comprehension checks
- a reading activity
- a writing activity

Unit Review Activity

list of the PCMs needed for that lesson. These unit-specific PCMs follow the lesson notes for each unit. Some of the PCMs will be used multiple times in the lessons, and multiple sets of other PCMs will be needed for some activities. Therefore, copying or pasting them onto card stock or other heavy paper is advisable.

The lessons also include suggestions for realia or authentic materials to use in explaining or enhancing lesson content and activities. These suggestions include real or instructor-made documents, visuals from newspapers or magazines, and real objects.

Central Theme Picture and Storyboard: In each unit, the PCMs begin with a theme picture, introduced in Lesson A: Life Skill. This theme picture provides the context for the lesson. It can also be used to assess prior knowledge or provide a link to the learners' backgrounds. Lesson B: Civic Responsibility begins, when appropriate, with a storyboard of four frames, used primarily to demonstrate the civics concept under discussion. This storyboard is also often woven into the lesson itself.

Vocabulary Cards: In all lessons, large vocabulary cards include a graphic representation, or picture cue, and a target word or phrase to be presented simultaneously. Some lessons also include a set of small picture cards with just the graphic representation and a set of small word cards. The word is first taught orally. The print form becomes "environmental print" while the instructor refers to the graphic in the lessons. Learners may use the picture cues in all activities to provide support. Later in the lesson, the print forms of the words or phrases are the focus of the optional reading and writing activities.

Activity Sheets: Reproducible activity sheets are provided for selected activities and may be completed as a group or by individual learners. Most activity sheets are presented orally. They stress graphic representations rather than written words, to help learners succeed regardless of their reading level or ability. Teachers may want to create enlarged versions of activity sheets for ease in modeling or reviewing activities.

Unit Review Activities for Assessment: Each unit includes a review activity that can be used to assess and provide a written record of learner progress. These unit reviews mirror the kinds of exercises learners have done throughout the lessons. They combine the life skill and the civic responsibility being taught. The term *Review* is used rather than *Assessment* to minimize learners' test anxiety.

Selected Teaching Techniques

The *Living in America* curriculum uses language-teaching techniques that research has shown to be appropriate for adult learners and effective with learners with limited or no prior exposure to English. The techniques suggested can be used with individuals or with groups of various sizes. They can also be modified for learners with more advanced abilities. Models and clear steps are provided within each activity to provide direction for the instructor.

Assessment of Prior Knowledge: Prior knowledge is assessed at the beginning of each lesson using the theme picture or the storyboard. The instructor points to elements of the picture that represent key themes in the lesson and gives learners time to make associations, name or point out objects, and preview new words.

Introduction of Target Vocabulary: Target, or core, vocabulary is practiced in each oral language activity. New words or terms are learned in the context of the theme picture or storyboard. Graphic representations of words, available on the vocabulary cards, are also effective tools for introducing vocabulary. Mime and/or gestures are used to model actions, elicit responses, or explain complex concepts when new vocabulary is difficult to represent graphically.

Modeling: Instructors are provided with suggestions and examples of how to model vocabulary within the context of each lesson. Modeling accurate pronunciation and usage is important for beginning ELLs.

Repetition: Repetition is the key to helping language learners develop quick, natural responses. Activity and exercise guidelines suggest repeating every word, phrase, and sentence pattern three times, or more if necessary. Learners repeat target vocabulary as a group before individuals are asked to produce the vocabulary on their own.

Dialogues: Short dialogues and role plays of two to four sentences are introduced within activities. Longer dialogues are often introduced to present conversation patterns or to develop understanding of a civics concept.

Gestures: Use gestures to indicate when the learners should listen, respond, stop, wait, or take turns. Use gestures consistently to provide nonverbal cues during lessons.

Backward Buildup: This technique is employed by breaking a target sentence into parts and starting with repetition of the last phrase. For example: *I am going / to the store / to buy milk.* Teach *to buy milk* first. When the learner can say *to buy milk,* teach *to the store.* Combine the two. Then teach *I am going.* Finally, model the entire sentence and have the learners repeat it as one unit.

Substitution: Teach a target pattern, and then replace a word or phrase with another that completes the sentence. For example: *He is her husband.* After the learner can say this sentence, replace the initial target, *husband,* with *brother.* For example:

> **I:** "He is her husband."
> **I:** "Brother."
> **L:** "He is her brother."

Error Correction: Correct only when a learner's answer does not convey the correct meaning. State the correct response and ask learners to restate the correct answer. For example, the learner is asked to indicate that the windshield is broken but responds with a reference to the tire.

> **I:** "What is broken?" (Point to windshield.)
> **L:** "The tire is broken."
> **I:** "Windshield. The windshield is broken." (Motion for the learner to repeat.)
> **L:** "The windshield is broken."

Modified Input: When the learner does not have the language facility to reproduce a complete sentence, speech can be modified by dropping articles, verbs, and inflectional endings. For example: *Windshield broken* or *Not OK.* With simplified grammar, the meaning is clearer to the learner. A learner response in modified speech or using a one-word answer would not be corrected, as long as the correct meaning is conveyed.

Reinforcement: Give immediate and genuine reinforcement when a learner gives a correct answer. Use words like *good, good work, OK, yes, right,* and *terrific.* Restatement of a correct answer is also a form of positive reinforcement.

Preparation for Using *Living in America*

Prior to implementing the *Living in America* curriculum, familiarize yourself with the lesson content. Preview each lesson, to make notes for quick reference and to gather or duplicate graphics, activity sheets, and additional materials needed for the lesson.

Many resources are available to instructors and learners in the field of ESL. Search local libraries or look online for materials that are appropriate for the level of ELLs being served and that contribute to professional development. A list of useful search topics is provided in the sidebar.

Useful Search Topics

- Adult Learners
- Civics Education
- EL-Civics
- English Language Learner (ELL)
- English as a Second Language (ESL)
- English for Speakers of Other Languages (ESOL)
- Immigrant Education
- Literacy
- Migrant Education
- ProLiteracy Worldwide
- Refugee Education
- Teaching English to Speakers of Other Languages (TESOL)

The *Living in America* Curriculum

Getting Along with Others
Introducing Yourself
Marking Your Calendar
Understanding Families
Protecting Yourself and Others
Understanding Manners in the U.S.

Using Official Documents
Using Money
Saving Necessary Documents
Finding Work
Preparing for Tax Time

Fitting into Your Community
Going to the Store
Recycling
Navigating the Community
Using the Phone
Paying for Phone Calls
Riding a Bicycle

Understanding Key Health Issues
Using Doctor and Hospital Services
Handling Dangerous Chemicals
Medicine and Controlled Substances
Having Safe Relationships

Operating a Motor Vehicle
Getting Ready to Drive
Driving
Owning a Car
Keeping Your Car Running
Maintaining Your Car
Navigating the Roads

Knowing Your Rights and Responsibilities
Getting a Lawyer
Communicating with Neighbors and the Police
Understanding Community Responsibilities
Understanding a Lease
Maintaining Housing

Getting a Lawyer

Finding Legal Services

VOCABULARY

NOUNS
Law

Lawyer

License

Recommendation

Yellow pages

ADJECTIVE
Illegal

VERB PHRASES
Break the law

Find a lawyer

Get recommendation

Look for license

Look at the yellow pages

Need a lawyer

Objective
To help learners understand how to find legal services in the event that legal counsel is necessary

Materials Included
- Central theme picture
- Large reproducible vocabulary cards
- Small reproducible picture cards
- Picture/Word Matching activity sheet
- Complete the Dialogue activity sheet
- **OK/Not OK** cards (page 250)

Materials Needed
- Additional instructor copy (enlarged) of the activity sheets to assist the learners
- A picture of a courtroom, including key people (judge, witness, lawyer(s), etc.)
- Local yellow pages

Central Theme Picture

Introduce the Theme Picture

1. Show learners the theme picture and ask for a response.
2. Encourage learners to say anything about the picture that they can.

> **I:** "What's happening in this picture?" (Point out key things about the picture to elicit a response.)

Oral Language Activity 1

Introduce the Target Nouns

1. Show each large noun card to the group while pronouncing each word slowly and clearly.

> **I:** "Law." (Hold up the **law** card and motion for the group to repeat the word together.)
>
> **G:** "Law."
>
> **I:** "Good. Law." (Hold up the **law** card. Motion for the group to repeat.)
>
> **G:** "Law."
>
> **I:** "Law." (Motion for the group to repeat. Put the **law** card at the front of the room.)
>
> **G:** "Law."

2. Introduce the other target nouns using the format above (**lawyer, license, recommendation,** and **yellow pages**).
3. Use mime, pictures, and realia as necessary to help the group understand the target nouns.
4. Say each word and have the group repeat each one three times.
5. Repeat any words more than three times as necessary.

Concentration Activity

1. Shuffle two sets of the small picture cards.
2. Spread cards out on a table or other visible surface facedown so that they are not overlapping.
3. Show learners how to do the activity by turning over two cards. Model one failure (no match) and one success (match).
4. Model getting a matched pair to show how a player with a matched pair keeps the cards and is allowed an extra turn.
5. Model getting cards that do not match to show how the cards should be put back facedown, at random, on the table.

6. Motion for learners to begin the activity by choosing the first person to start.
7. Have each learner choose two cards and identify them.
8. Assist learners as needed.
9. Motion for the learners to hold up each pair of cards and identify them at the end of the activity.
10. Count each learner's pairs (and encourage the group to count along).

Comprehension Check

1. Collect the target noun cards and reshuffle them.
2. Introduce the cards one by one, identifying the nouns correctly and incorrectly at random.
3. Model how to say Yes when the card is correctly identified, and No when it is incorrectly identified.

> **I:** "Yellow pages." (Hold up the **yellow pages** card.)
>
> **I:** "Yellow pages. Yes." (Point to the **yellow pages** card and nod in agreement. Motion for the learners to repeat.)
>
> **G:** "Yes."
>
> **I:** "Lawyer." (Hold up the **yellow pages** card again.)
>
> **I:** "Lawyer. No." (Point to the **yellow pages** card and shake head in disagreement. Motion for the learners to repeat.)
>
> **G:** "No."

4. Continue with other target nouns at random.
5. Repeat words as necessary.

Oral Language Activity 2

Introduce the Target Verb Phrases and Adjective

1. Show each large verb phrase card and adjective card to the group while pronouncing each word slowly and clearly.

> **I:** "Look at yellow pages." (Hold up the **look at yellow pages** card and mime the action using a copy of the local yellow pages. Motion for the group to repeat.)
>
> **G:** "Look at yellow pages."
>
> **I:** "Good. Look at yellow pages." (Motion for the group to repeat.)
>
> **G:** "Look at yellow pages."
>
> **I:** "Look at yellow pages." (Motion for the group to repeat. Put the **look at yellow pages** card at the front of the room.)
>
> **G:** "Look at yellow pages."

2. Introduce the other verb phrases using the format on the previous page (**break the law, need a lawyer, find a lawyer, look for license,** and **get recommendation**).
3. Demonstrate the word **illegal** by using clear examples that the group is already familiar with (see suggestions below) to teach this concept.

Suggestions for Teaching *illegal*

Stealing = illegal
Paying for items in a store = legal
Wearing a seatbelt = legal
Not wearing a seatbelt = illegal

4. Say each word or phrase and have the group repeat each one three times.
5. Repeat any terms more than three times as necessary.

Match the Verb Phrases Activity

1. Hold up each verb phrase card for the group and ask the learners to repeat the terms in the order suggested by the combinations below.

> **I:** "Break the law." (Hold up the **break the law** card and motion for the group to repeat the phrase.)
> **G:** "Break the law."
> **I:** "Break the law." (Hold up the **break the law** card and motion for the group to repeat the phrase.)
> **G:** "Break the law."
> **I:** "Break the law." (Hold up the **break the law** card and motion for the group to repeat the phrase.)
> **G:** "Break the law."

Combinations

Break the law - need a lawyer
Find a lawyer - get recommendation
Find a lawyer - look at yellow pages
Find a lawyer - look for license

2. Hold up the **need a lawyer** card, review the phrase using the format above, and associate the phrase and card with the **break the law** card.
3. Repeat the format above with the other combinations of phrases.
4. Reshuffle the cards and hold them up. Ask the learners to identify them verbally.

5. Lay the cards faceup on the table or other visible surface that learners can easily reach. Have the group pair the cards and place them in the order that was presented by the activity.
6. Assist learners as necessary.

Comprehension Check

1. Shuffle all of the verb phrase cards together.
2. Distribute the cards to the learners at random, so that each learner has one card.
3. Call out each verb phrase and motion for the learner(s) with the corresponding card to hold it up.
4. Continue calling out target verb phrases and motioning for learners to hold up the corresponding cards.
5. Assist learners as necessary.

Oral Language Activity 3

Review of the Target Vocabulary

1. Place the large vocabulary cards in a visible location at the front of the room.
2. Point to each card or hold cards up one by one. Prompt the group to identify the card. Demonstrate the verb phrases to prompt learners' responses.

> **I:** "What's this?" (Point to the **lawyer** card and motion for the group to respond.)
> **G:** "Lawyer."
> **I:** "What's this?" (Demonstrate looking at the yellow pages. Point to the **yellow pages** card and motion for the group to respond.)
> **G:** "Look at yellow pages."
> **I:** "What's this?" (Point to the **illegal** card and motion for the group to respond.)
> **G:** "Illegal."

3. Have the group identify all target vocabulary using the format above.
4. Assist learners as necessary.

Tap Activity

1. Shuffle two sets of large vocabulary cards together. Spread out one complete set faceup on a table or other surface so that the cards are not crowded together or overlapping.
2. Distribute an instructor-devised tapper to each learner.

MATERIALS

Large vocabulary cards (two sets)

Local yellow pages

Instructor-devised tapper (one per learner and one for instructor)

OK/Not OK cards (one set per learner and one set for instructor)

NOTE

As an addition to this lesson, instructors can help learners understand that, depending on the community, pro bono legal assistance may be accessed through advocacy or other nonprofit organizations.

3. Use the combinations presented in Oral Language Activity 2 to establish which cards should be held up to prompt the learners to tap the correct corresponding card.
4. Demonstrate the activity using an example from the combinations below.
5. Hold up both cards and verbally identify only the first card in each set.
6. Show learners how to look for and tap the card on the table that corresponds to the second card held up.

Combinations

Instructor identifies	Learners tap
Break the law	Need a lawyer
Find a lawyer	Get recommendation
Find a lawyer	Look at yellow pages
Find a lawyer	Look for license

7. Motion for the learners to listen carefully by holding one hand up with palm open to an ear.
8. Hold up a combination of cards. Call out the first phrase. Ask learners to look for the corresponding card on the table and identify it with a tapper.
9. Motion for the learners to hold up their tappers to begin.

> **I:** "Ready?" (Hold the tapper up.)
> **G:** "OK."
> **I:** "Break the law." (Hold up the **break the law** card with the **need a lawyer** card. Motion for the learners to try to quickly identify the corresponding card and tap it.)

10. Ask the learner whose tapper identifies the correct card first to pick the card up and repeat the phrase it represents. The learner keeps the card.

> **L:** "Need a lawyer." (Learner holds up the **need a lawyer** card.)

11. When all of the cards have been removed from the table, have each learner identify which cards he or she holds.
12. Repeat this activity more than once to help ensure comprehension and verbal practice.
13. Assist learners as necessary.

Comprehension Check

1. Distribute **OK/Not OK** cards to each learner.
2. Hold up pairs of cards from Oral Language Activity 3 that are correct combinations and pairs that are incorrect.

3. Ask learners to associate the **OK** card with correct combinations and the **Not OK** card with incorrect combinations.

> **I:** "Break the law. Need a lawyer." (Hold up the **break the law** and **need a lawyer** cards.)
>
> **I:** "Break the law. Need a lawyer. Yes." (Hold up the **OK** card. Motion for the group to hold up the **OK** card.)
>
> **G:** "Yes." (Learners should hold up the **OK** card.)
>
> **I:** "Break the law. Look for license." (Hold up the **break the law** and **look for license** cards.)
>
> **I:** "Break the law. Look for license. No." (Hold up the **Not OK** card. Motion for the group to hold up the **Not OK** card.)
>
> **G:** "No." (Learners should hold up the **Not OK** card.)

Oral Language Activity 4

Introduce the Dialogue

1. Write the sample dialogue (see example below) on the board or on chart paper.
2. Refer to the lines in the dialogue by pointing to each line as it is presented with corresponding cards.

> **Speaker 1:** "Break the law." (Hold up the **break the law** and **illegal** cards and motion for a response.)
>
> **Speaker 2:** "Illegal."
>
> **Speaker 1:** "What should you do?" (Hold up the **find a lawyer** card and motion for a response.)
>
> **Speaker 2:** "Find a lawyer."
>
> **Speaker 1:** "What should you do?" (Hold up the **look at yellow pages** card and motion for a response.)
>
> **Speaker 2:** "Look at yellow pages."
>
> **Speaker 1:** "What should you do?" (Hold up the **get a recommendation** card and motion for a response.)
>
> **Speaker 2:** "Get a recommendation."

3. Make sure that the learners can respond to each card before continuing on to the next activity.

Dialogue Activity

1. Perform the dialogue (see example on the next page) with the instructor taking the role of Speaker 1 and learners taking the role of Speaker 2.
2. Assist learners through their lines, using gestures and vocabulary cards to prompt them.

Speaker 1:	"Break the law." (Hold up the **break the law** and **illegal** cards. Motion for a response.)
Speaker 2:	"Illegal." (Learners should point to the **illegal** card held by the instructor.)
Speaker 1:	"What should you do?" (Hold up the **find a lawyer** card and motion for a response.)
Speaker 2:	"Find a lawyer."
Speaker 1:	"What should you do?" (Hold up the **look at yellow pages** card and motion for a response.)
Speaker 2:	"Look at yellow pages."
Speaker 1:	"What should you do?" (Hold up the **get a recommendation** card and motion for a response.)
Speaker 2:	"Get a recommendation."

3. Point to each word whenever the dialogue is repeated in this activity.
4. Perform the dialogue with the instructor as Speaker 1 and the group responding as Speaker 2 to the instructor's lines and prompts.
5. Perform the dialogue as a group three times. Assist the group as necessary.

Comprehension Check

1. Hold up two different vocabulary cards for the group.
2. Identify one of the cards and ask the learners to point to the correct one.

| I: | "Lawyer." (Hold up the **look in yellow pages** and **lawyer** cards. Ask the learners to point to the correct card and identify it.) |
| G: | "Lawyer." (Learners should point to the **lawyer** card.) |

3. Repeat the check with varying pairs to help ensure learners' understanding of the vocabulary.

Reading Activity

MATERIALS

Large noun cards

Picture/Word Matching activity sheet (one enlarged and one per learner)

Review

1. Shuffle all of the target noun cards.
2. Show each card to the group while pronouncing each word slowly and clearly.
3. Run a finger under each word to help learners begin to recognize the words apart from the pictures.
4. Have the learners repeat the words at least three times.

> **I:** "Law." (Point to the word.)
>
> **G:** "Law."
>
> **I:** "Law." (Underline the word with a finger. Motion for the group to repeat the word.)
>
> **G:** "Law."

NOTE

Separating words from pictures should be done gradually and after plenty of practice.

5. Continue to review with the cards, using the pattern above.
6. Fold cards in half to show only the words, to help learners become less dependent on the pictures.
7. Move from group to individual practice as learners become more comfortable reading the words without the assistance of the pictures.

Picture/Word Matching Activity

1. Pass out a Picture/Word Matching activity sheet to each learner.
2. Place a set of pictures and words matched correctly in a visible location, to assist learners.
3. Post an enlarged copy of the activity sheet in the front of the room.
4. On the enlarged activity sheet, use the example to show learners how to complete the activity.
5. Point to the first picture and ask learners to identify it.
6. Find the word that corresponds to the first picture and show learners how the line connects the picture and the word.

> **I:** "License." (Motion for learners to look at the words. Gesture looking for the word *license*.)
>
> **I:** "Here it is. License." (Trace the line between the picture and the corresponding word.)

7. Point to each picture and have learners identify each one verbally.
8. Have learners find the word or phrase that corresponds to each picture and draw a line from the picture to the corresponding word or phrase.
9. Encourage learners to refer to the set of matched cards for assistance.
10. Have learners complete their activity sheets.

Writing Activity

© New Readers Press. All rights reserved.

MATERIALS

Large vocabulary cards

Complete the Dialogue activity sheet (one enlarged and one per learner)

NOTE

Separating words from pictures should be done gradually and after plenty of practice.

Review

1. Shuffle all of the target vocabulary cards together.
2. Show each card to the group while pronouncing each word slowly and clearly.
3. Run a finger under each word to help learners begin to recognize the words apart from the pictures.
4. Have the learners repeat the words at least three times.

> **I:** "Lawyer." (Point to the word.)
> **G:** "Lawyer."
> **I:** "Lawyer." (Underline the word with a finger. Motion for the group to repeat the word.)
> **G:** "Lawyer."

5. Continue to review with the cards, using the pattern above.
6. Fold cards in half to show only the words, to help learners become less dependent on the pictures.
7. Move from group to individual practice as learners become more comfortable reading the words without the assistance of the pictures.

Complete the Dialogue Activity

1. Distribute a Complete the Dialogue activity sheet to each learner.
2. Post an enlarged activity sheet in the front of the room.
3. Place the large vocabulary cards in a visible location, to assist learners.
4. Show the group how to use the pictures on the activity sheet to help complete the dialogue.
5. Identify one of the pictures and read the complete line, including the word or phrase corresponding to the picture.
6. Model for learners how to write the word or phrase on the line(s) next to the picture.
7. Have the learners write the missing words in the dialogue by referring to the vocabulary cards.
8. Assist learners as necessary.
9. Go through the completed dialogue verbally, with the instructor taking the part of Speaker 1 and learners taking the part of Speaker 2.

Right to an Attorney

VOCABULARY

NOUNS

Client

Court

Crime

Legal assistance

VERBS

Ask

Have a right

Help

Need

Objective

To help learners understand that they have a right to legal counsel

Materials Included

- Large reproducible vocabulary cards
- Small reproducible picture cards
- Picture Bingo boards
- Word Search activity sheet
- Fill in the Missing Words activity sheet
- **OK/Not OK** cards (page 250)

Materials Needed

- Additional instructor copy (enlarged) of the activity sheets to assist the learners
- Pictures of various crimes (e.g., a robbery, illegal drug use)
- A picture of a courtroom, including key people (judge, defendant, witness, lawyer(s), etc.), and a lawyer's office, including a lawyer and a client
- Small objects (buttons, coins, dry beans, etc.) to use as Bingo board markers

Civics Introduction

Right to an Attorney

Lawyers are especially important when an individual has legal trouble or has been accused of a crime. Individuals residing in the U.S. have the right to legal counsel. In situations where an individual cannot afford a lawyer, one is appointed to that person free of charge. A lawyer represents the best interests of the client before, during, and after a court trial and helps ensure that nothing infringes upon the rights of his or her client.

As presented in Lesson A, learners can find a lawyer through recommendations from friends or colleagues and/or from the yellow pages of a local telephone book. It is always important to confirm that a lawyer is a licensed professional before hiring legal counsel. It is also important to determine that a lawyer has experience in the area of law involved in an individual's case. Immigrant advocacy groups and local bar associations or legal aid agencies can be useful in getting recommendations or checking a lawyer's qualifications.

This topic is of special importance to newly arrived, non-English-speaking adults because they may not be aware of their right to legal counsel, especially their right to have a lawyer represent their interests in court. Furthermore, they may not be aware of reliable sources of recommendations or of pro bono counsel. Individuals residing in the U.S. need to understand how to find a licensed, well-qualified lawyer. They also need to understand that they can have a lawyer appointed by the court if they cannot afford legal counsel themselves.

Oral Language Activity 1

MATERIALS

Large noun cards (from Lessons A & B)

Small noun cards (from Lessons A & B)

Pictures of a courtroom, a law office, and the people in those places

Pictures showing various crimes

Bingo boards and Bingo board markers

OK/Not OK cards

Introduce the Target Nouns

1. Hold up a noun card and pronounce each word slowly and clearly.
2. Motion for learners to repeat each word.
3. Use pictures and mime as necessary to connect each noun with the learners' prior knowledge.

> **I:** "Client." (Hold up the **client** card. Motion for the group to repeat.)
>
> **G:** "Client."
>
> **I:** "Client." (Point to a learner in the room and use the **lawyer** card from Lesson A to express the meaning of **client.** Motion for the group to repeat.)
>
> **G:** "Client."
>
> **I:** "Client." (Hold up the **client** and **lawyer** cards. Motion for the group to repeat.)
>
> **G:** "Client."

4. Use the large vocabulary cards to introduce the other target nouns (**court, crime,** and **legal assistance**).
5. Use the **Not OK** card when introducing the term **crime** so that learners understand the consequences.
6. Have learners repeat each word at least three times.
7. Repeat pronunciation and practice the words more than three times as necessary.
8. Review nouns from Lesson A, which are included in the Picture Bingo Activity.

NOTE

Five marked boxes in a row horizontally, vertically, or diagonally = Bingo.

Picture Bingo Activity

1. Distribute one Bingo board and a set of Bingo markers to each learner.
2. Use the small noun cards to prompt the learners.
3. Put the small cards in an envelope or basket and mix them together.
4. Draw a card and identify it verbally, showing the card to the group.
5. Have learners mark any pictures on their boards corresponding to each noun card drawn.
6. Have each learner take a turn drawing a card and identifying the word or phrase pictured.
7. Have the entire group repeat each vocabulary term after the card is drawn.
8. Show the learners that the goal of the activity is to mark five boxes in a row, horizontally, vertically, or diagonally.

9. Ask the learners to call out *Bingo* if they have five boxes in a row marked.
10. Rotate the Bingo boards and do the activity again for additional practice.

Comprehension Check

1. Hold up two different cards and identify one of them correctly.
2. Have the group point to the card that was identified.
3. Motion for the group to repeat the word.
4. Continue the check with other pairs of noun cards.

> **I:** "Crime." (Hold up the **crime** and **court** cards. Motion for a response.)
>
> **G:** "Crime." (Learners point to the **crime** card.)

5. Ask the group if crime is OK or Not OK.

Oral Language Activity 2

MATERIALS

Large noun and verb cards

Lawyer card

Need a lawyer card from Lesson A

Introduce the Target Verbs and Phrases

1. Hold up each verb card and pronounce each word slowly and clearly motioning for learners to repeat each word.

> **I:** "Ask." (Hold up the **ask** card. Motion for the group to repeat.)
>
> **G:** "Ask."
>
> **I:** "Ask." (Hold up the **ask** card. Put a question mark on the board. Demonstrate the verb by asking learners simple questions (e.g., *What is your name? Where do you live?*). Motion for the group to repeat the verb.)
>
> **G:** "Ask."
>
> **I:** "Ask." (Hold up the **ask** card. Motion for the group to repeat.)
>
> **G:** "Ask."

2. Use mime and objects in the classroom as necessary to convey the meaning of each verb.
3. Use the large vocabulary cards to introduce the other target verbs and phrases (**have a right, help,** and **need**).
4. Have learners repeat each word at least three times.
5. Repeat pronunciation and practice the words more than three times as necessary.

Combine Nouns and Verbs Activity

1. Hold up combinations of nouns and verbs to introduce phrases. Present them in the sequence below, reflecting the order in which they would occur.
2. Say each phrase, pronouncing each word in the phrase slowly and clearly.

Sequence of Phrases

Need lawyer

Have a right to a lawyer

Ask help for legal assistance

I: "Need lawyer." (Hold up the **need** and **lawyer** cards. Motion for the group to repeat.)

G: "Need lawyer."

3. Have the group repeat each phrase at least three times.
4. Use mime and gestures to help convey the meaning of each phrase. Use the **Need a lawyer** card from Lesson A to reinforce that concept.
5. Shuffle all the vocabulary cards together. Lay them faceup at random on a table or other surface.
6. Model the activity by looking through the cards. Pick out a set of cards that will build one of the phrases practiced above.
7. Have learners group the cards to create phrases, then place the sets of cards in the correct sequence as presented above.
8. Assist learners as necessary.

Comprehension Check

1. Place the noun and verb cards, combined to represent phrases, in the correct sequence on a table or other available surface.
2. Ask learners to listen carefully by holding a palm open up to an ear.
3. Motion for learners to point to the cards representing the phrases as they are called out and to repeat the phrase that was called out.

I: "Have a right to a lawyer." (Motion for the group to point to the correct phrase and repeat it.)

G: "Have a right to a lawyer." (Learners should point to the **have a right** and **lawyer** cards.)

I: "Need lawyer." (Motion for the group to point to the correct phrase and repeat it.)

G: "Need lawyer." (Learners should point to the **need** and **lawyer** cards.)

4. Continue calling out other phrases and asking learners to point to the correct phrase.

Oral Language Activity 3

MATERIALS

Large noun cards

Large verb cards

Lawyer card from Lesson A

Introduce the Concept Development Activity

1. On the board or on chart paper, post individual cards or combinations of noun and verb cards in the order presented in the dialogue below.
2. Pronounce each word or phrase slowly and clearly.

> **I:** "Crime." (Point to the **crime** card. Motion for the group to repeat.)
>
> **G:** "Crime."
>
> **I:** "Need lawyer." (Point to the **need** and **lawyer** cards and motion for the group to repeat.)
>
> **G:** "Need lawyer."
>
> **I:** "Have a right to lawyer." (Point to the **have a right** and **lawyer** cards. Motion for the group to repeat.)
>
> **G:** "Have a right to lawyer."
>
> **I:** "Ask help for legal assistance." (Point to the **ask, help,** and **legal assistance** cards. Motion for the group to repeat.)
>
> **G:** "Ask help for legal assistance."
>
> **I:** "Court." (Point to the **court** card. Motion for the group to repeat.)
>
> **G:** "Court."

3. Have learners repeat each phrase at least three times.
4. Repeat pronunciation and practice the phrases more than three times as necessary.

Concept Development Activity

1. Connect together noun and verb cards to create each of the target phrases, using tape, string, or other instructor-devised method.
2. Mix together the individual noun cards and the phrases created in step 1, and place them in random order on the table or other available surface.
3. Ask the learners to place the phrases in the correct order as presented in the Introduce activity (see sequence below).
4. Assist learners as necessary.

> ### Correct Order of Phrases
>
> 1. Crime
> 2. Need lawyer
> 3. Have a right to a lawyer
> 4. Ask help for legal assistance
> 5. Court

Comprehension Check

1. Shuffle the cards for the phrases used in Oral Language Activity 3.
2. Distribute the cards to learners or pairs of learners at random.
3. Call out each target phrase and motion for the learner(s) with the corresponding card(s) to hold them up.
4. Continue calling out target phrases and motioning for learners to hold up the corresponding cards.
5. Repeat the comprehension check using the correct order established in Oral Language Activity 3.
6. Assist learners as necessary.

Oral Language Activity 4

Materials

Large noun cards

Large verb cards

Yes/No cards

OK/Not OK cards (one set per learner)

NOTE

Pointing to the words while reading is important to do even if the learners are non-readers or nonliterate.

Introduce the Dialogue

1. Write the sample dialogue (see example below) on the board or on chart paper.
2. Combine vocabulary cards to practice target phrases in the dialogue.
3. Use the format below to introduce the appropriate sequence for the dialogue.

> **Speaker 1:** "What do you need?" (Hold up the **crime** card. Motion for the group to respond.)
>
> **Speaker 2:** "Need lawyer."
>
> **Speaker 1:** "What right do you have?" (Hold up the **lawyer** card. Motion for the group to respond.)
>
> **Speaker 2:** "Have right to lawyer."
>
> **Speaker 1:** "What do you do?" (Hold up the **legal assistance** card. Motion for the group to respond.)
>
> **Speaker 2:** "Ask help for legal assistance."

4. Introduce the dialogue, with the instructor taking the role of Speaker 1 and the learners taking the role of Speaker 2.
5. Make sure that the learners can respond to each question and visual prompt correctly before continuing on to the dialogue activity.

Dialogue Activity

1. Perform the dialogue, with the instructor taking the role of Speaker 1 and the learners taking the role of Speaker 2.
2. Assist learners through their lines using gestures and vocabulary cards to prompt their responses.

> **Speaker 1:** "What do you need?" (Hold up the **crime** card. Motion for the group to respond.)
>
> **Speaker 2:** "Need lawyer."
>
> **Speaker 1:** "What right do you have?" (Hold up the **lawyer** card. Motion for the group to respond.)
>
> **Speaker 2:** "Have right to lawyer."
>
> **Speaker 1:** "What do you do?" (Hold up the **legal assistance** card. Motion for the group to respond.)
>
> **Speaker 2:** "Ask help for legal assistance."

3. Perform the dialogue as a group three times.
4. If needed, model the responses and have learners repeat.
5. Point to each word whenever the dialogue is repeated in this activity.
6. Assist the group as necessary.

Comprehension Check

1. Distribute a set of **OK/Not OK** cards to each learner.
2. Hold up word or phrase cards at random with a **Yes** or **No** card.
3. Ask the group to say OK or Not OK and hold up the correct card in response to the combination displayed.

> **I:** "Right to lawyer. Yes." (Motion for a response.)
>
> **G:** "OK." (Learners should hold up the **OK** card.)
>
> **I:** "Right to lawyer. No." (Motion for a response.)
>
> **G:** "Not OK." (Learners should hold up the **Not OK** card.)

4. Assist learners as necessary.

Reading Activity

MATERIALS

Large noun cards

Large verb cards

Word Search activity sheet (one enlarged and one per learner)

Review

1. Shuffle the large noun and verb cards.
2. Show each card to the group while pronouncing each word slowly and clearly.
3. Run a finger under each word to help learners begin to recognize the words apart from the pictures.
4. Have the learners repeat the words at least three times.

> **I:** "Crime." (Point to the word.)
> **G:** "Crime."
> **I:** "Crime." (Underline the word with a finger. Motion for the group to repeat the word.)
> **G:** "Crime."

NOTE

Separating words from pictures should be done gradually and after plenty of practice.

5. Continue to review with the cards, using the pattern above.
6. Fold cards in half to show only the words, to help learners become less dependent on the pictures.
7. Move from group to individual practice as learners become more comfortable reading the words without the assistance of the pictures.

Word Search Activity Sheet

1. Pass out a Word Search activity sheet to each learner.
2. Post an enlarged copy of the activity sheet in the front of the room or other visible location.
3. Using the enlarged activity sheet, show the learners how to use the pictures and words listed at the top of the activity sheet to locate words in the word search.
4. Choose a word from the list to locate in the word search.
5. Read the word for the learners and point to the picture that represents it.
6. Demonstrate how to look in the word search for the word written under the picture.
7. Model for learners how to circle each word in the word search when it is found.
8. Have the learners say each word from the list before they begin to search. Have learners complete their own sheets.
9. Assist learners as necessary.
10. Check answers by having learners come up and circle the words on the enlarged activity sheet.

Writing Activity

MATERIALS

Large noun cards

Large verb cards

Lawyer card from Lesson A

Fill in the Missing Words activity sheet (one enlarged and one per learner)

OK/Not OK cards

Review

1. Shuffle the large noun and verb cards.
2. Show each card to the group while pronouncing each word slowly and clearly.
3. Run a finger under each word to help learners begin to recognize the words apart from the pictures.
4. Have the learners repeat the words at least three times.

I:	"Legal assistance." (Point to the words.)
G:	"Legal assistance."
I:	"Legal assistance." (Underline the words with a finger. Motion for the group to repeat the words.)
G:	"Legal assistance."

NOTE

Separating words from pictures should be done gradually and after plenty of practice.

5. Continue to review with the cards, using the pattern above.
6. Fold cards in half to show only the words, to help learners become less dependent on the pictures.
7. Move from group to individual practice as learners become more comfortable reading the words without the assistance of the pictures.

Fill in the Missing Words Activity Sheet

1. Place the large noun and verb cards, including the **Lawyer** card from Lesson A, in a visible location.
2. Post an enlarged copy of the activity sheet in the front of the room.
3. Pass out a Fill in the Missing Words activity sheet to each learner.
4. Demonstrate how the group can use the posted cards to help them fill in the missing information on the activity sheet.
5. On the enlarged activity sheet, use the example in item 3 to model for learners how to write the correct word or phrase on the line(s) next to each picture.
6. Assist learners as necessary.

Unit Review Activity

MATERIALS

Unit Review activity sheet (one enlarged and one per learner)

Large vocabulary cards (from Lessons A & B)

NOTE

The Unit Review Activity can be done as a group activity for reinforcing the concepts learned in the lesson or done as an individual activity for assessment purposes.

OK or Not OK Review Activity

1. Use the large vocabulary cards from Lessons A and B to review the vocabulary and concepts of the unit.
2. Post an enlarged copy of the activity sheet in the front of the room or in another visible location.
3. Point to each picture on the enlarged activity sheet and ask learners to identify it. Make sure learners understand the symbol for No (circle with slash) to indicate that what is pictured is not available.
4. Distribute a copy of the Unit Review Activity sheet to each learner.
5. On the enlarged activity sheet, point to the picture or set of pictures in each item. Elicit from learners whether the action or combination in the item is OK (desirable, legal, or an appropriate action) or Not OK (not desirable, illegal, or an unwise action).
6. Ask learners to complete the activity on their own sheets. If necessary, use the enlarged activity sheet to model for learners how to check the correct column to indicate that the item is OK or Not OK.

Central Theme Picture

Unit 1 *Getting a Lawyer* Lesson A *Life Skill*

Law

Large Vocabulary Cards

Lawyer

Large Vocabulary Cards

Recommendation

Unit 1 *Getting a Lawyer* Lesson A *Life Skill*

License

Large Vocabulary Cards

Unit 1 *Getting a Lawyer* Lesson A *Life Skill*

Yellow pages

Illegal

Find a lawyer

Break the law

Get recommendation

Look for license

Need a lawyer

Look at the yellow pages

Unit 1 *Getting a Lawyer* Lesson A   Small Picture Cards

Unit 1 *Getting a Lawyer* Lesson A   Small Picture Cards

Unit 1 *Getting a Lawyer* Lesson A   Small Picture Cards

Unit 1 *Getting a Lawyer* Lesson A   Small Picture Cards

Unit 1 *Getting a Lawyer* Lesson A   Small Picture Cards

Picture/Word Matching Activity

Look at the pictures and words. Draw a line from the picture to the correct word(s).

1.

2.

3.

4.

5.

Law

Yellow pages

Recommendation

License

Lawyer

Complete the Dialogue

Look at the pictures. Write the missing word(s). Complete the dialogue.

1. Speaker 1: Break the _____.
   Speaker 2: _____.

2. Speaker 1: What should you do?
   Speaker 2: Find a _____.

3. Speaker 1: What should you do?
   Speaker 2: Look at _____.

4. Speaker 1: What should you do?
   Speaker 2: Get a _____.

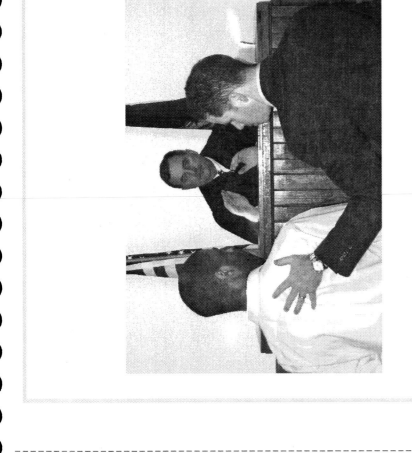

Court

Client

Crime

✂ -

Legal assistance

Have a right

Ask

Help

Need

Unit 1 *Getting a Lawyer* Lesson B   Small Picture Cards

Unit 1 *Getting a Lawyer* Lesson B   Small Picture Cards

Unit 1 *Getting a Lawyer* Lesson B   Small Picture Cards

Unit 1 *Getting a Lawyer* Lesson B   Small Picture Cards

Picture Bingo Board 1

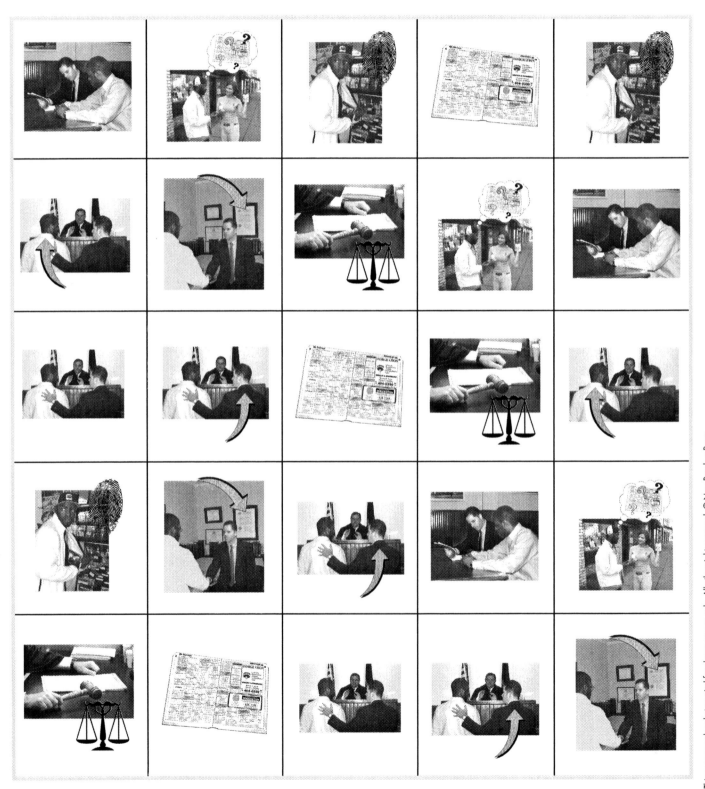

Picture Bingo Board 2

Picture Bingo Board 3

Picture Bingo Board 4

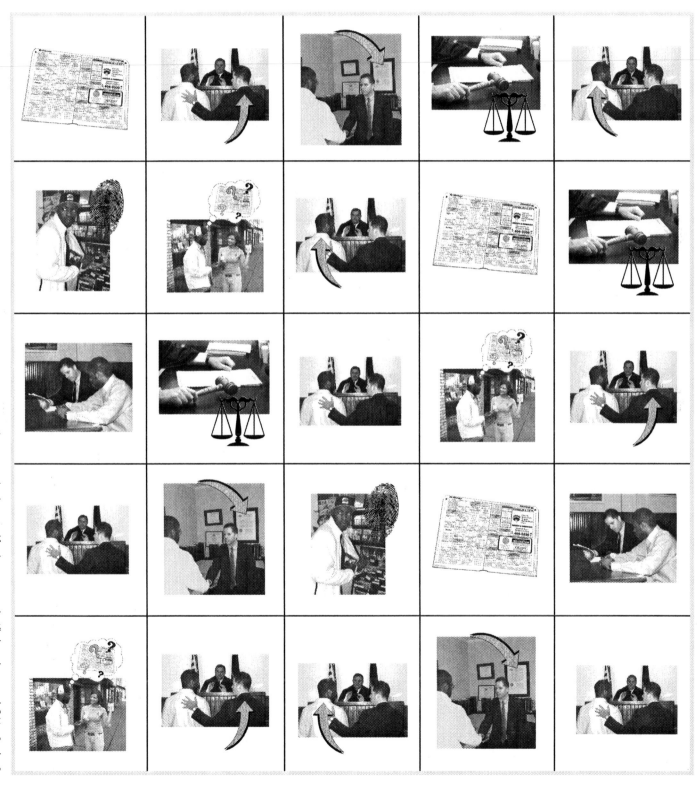

Word Search Activity

Look at the pictures. Find the words in the puzzle. Circle the words.

Client **Court** **Crime** **Legal assistance**

a	t	f	l	o	p	b	u	u	c	d	l	o	r	h
t	x	j	l	c	r	i	m	e	j	k	b	s	n	n
e	f	h	n	u	b	h	n	a	c	l	i	e	n	t
d	f	j	s	f	g	a	l	k	n	z	d	r	k	r
l	e	g	a	l	a	s	s	i	s	t	a	n	c	e
x	g	x	d	o	u	f	y	u	o	p	w	p	a	l
q	z	o	t	s	t	c	o	u	r	t	k	u	n	s
a	m	u	t	h	t	e	s	h	p	e	y	k	d	o

Fill in the Missing Words Activity

Look at the pictures. Write the correct word(s).

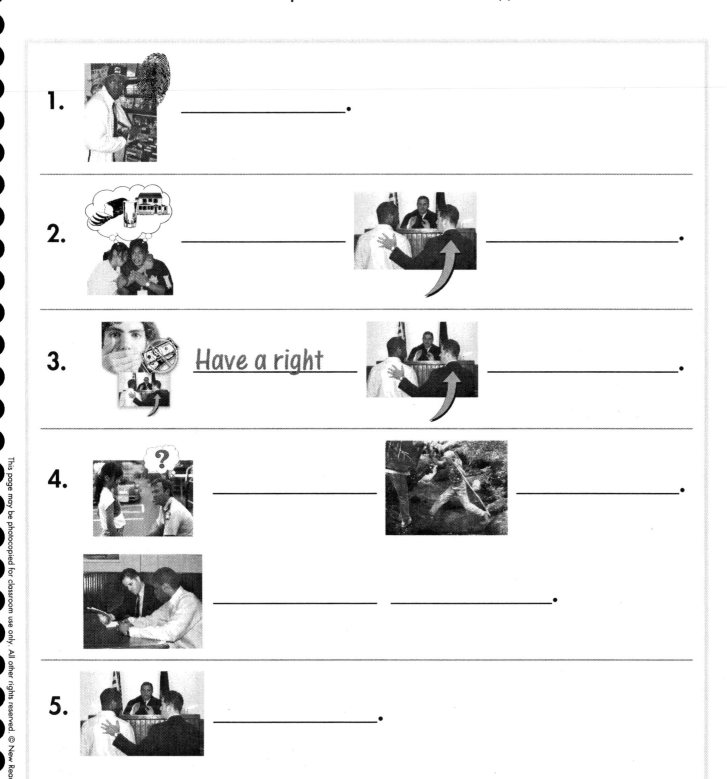

1. _____.

2. _____ _____.

3. <u>Have a right</u> _____.

4. _____ _____.

_____ _____.

5. _____.

Look at the pictures. Check OK or Not OK.

		OK	Not OK
		___	___
		___	___
		___	___
		___	___
		___	___
		___	___

Unit 2

Communicating with Neighbors and the Police

Lesson A - Life Skill

Social Skills

VOCABULARY

PHRASES

Hello.

How are you?

Fine, thanks.

Nice to meet you.

Nice to meet you, too.

What's your name?

My name is Maria.

Where are you from?

Mexico.

Goodbye.

NOTE

The name *Maria* is underlined on the **My name is** card to indicate that this slot can be changed. Learners should be taught to respond with their own names when prompted with that vocabulary card.

Objective

To help learners understand basic greetings and small talk commonly used when meeting others in the community

Materials Included

- Central theme picture
- Large reproducible vocabulary cards
- Small reproducible picture cards
- Small reproducible word cards
- Matching activity sheet
- Dialogue Writing activity sheet
- **Yes/No** cards

Materials Needed

- Soft ball or other tossable object
- Additional instructor copy (enlarged) of the activity sheets
- Large map of the world
- Pictures of people meeting and talking

Central Theme Picture

MATERIALS

Theme picture

POSSIBLE RESPONSES

Man

Officer

Paper

Police

Talk

Introduce the Theme Picture

1. Show learners the theme picture and ask for a response.
2. Encourage learners to say anything about the picture that they can.

> **I:** "What's happening in this picture?" (Point out key things about the picture to elicit a response.)

Oral Language Activity 1

MATERIALS

Large phrase cards (selected cards as specified in activity)

Pictures of people meeting and talking

Soft ball or other tossable object

Yes/No cards

Introduce Common Greetings

1. Show each selected phrase card to the group **(Hello., How are you?, Fine, thanks., What's your name?, My name is _____.).** Pronounce each word slowly and clearly.
2. Show pictures of people meeting and talking to each other, to establish the context for this activity.

> **I:** "Hello." (Hold up the **hello** card. Motion for the group to repeat.)
> **G:** "Hello."
> **I:** "Good. Hello." (Motion for the group to repeat.)
> **G:** "Hello."
> **I:** "Hello." (Motion for the group to repeat. Put the **hello** card at the front of the room.)
> **G:** "Hello."

3. Introduce the target phrases using the format above.
4. Say each phrase and have the group repeat each one three times.
5. Repeat any terms more than three times as necessary.

Zigzag Ball Toss

1. Divide the group in half.
2. Place learners in two lines so that each person faces a partner in the other line.
3. Demonstrate the activity with a partner.
4. Use a ball or other tossable object.
5. Perform the dialogue with the two lines of learners, one taking the part of Speaker 1 and the other Speaker 2.

6. Model each line of the dialogue and have learners repeat. Then model the parts of the dialogue for each line of learners and have those learners repeat.

> **Speaker 1:** "Hello."
> **Speaker 2:** "Hello."
> **Speaker 1:** "What's your name?"
> **Speaker 2:** "My name is Juan."
> **Speaker 1:** "How are you?"
> **Speaker 2:** "Fine, thanks."

7. Practice the dialogue as a group at least three times.
8. Direct learners to pass the ball back and forth and perform the dialogue in pairs.
9. Have the first learner in one line greet a partner in the other line, using the role of Speaker 1 in the sample dialogue, and then toss the ball to the partner, who responds in the role of Speaker 2.
10. The second learner can toss the ball back to his or her partner or to another learner in the first line. This will begin the zigzag ball toss. Whoever gets the ball then responds with the next part of the dialogue and tosses the ball to another partner.
11. Learners should continue tossing the ball back and forth, continuing through the dialogue. Once the dialogue is completed, learners can continue tossing the ball and repeat the dialogue.
12. Make sure each learner has a chance to practice the dialogue, assisting the group as necessary.
13. Once learners have performed the dialogue in their original roles, have them switch roles and repeat the ball toss.

NOTE

For this activity, learners will need to understand and be able to distinguish between the words Yes and No.

Comprehension Check

1. Collect the phrase cards from Oral Language Activity 1 and reshuffle them.
2. Review the cards one by one. Hold up each card and identify the phrases correctly and incorrectly at random.
3. Model how to say Yes when the card is correctly identified, and No when it is incorrectly identified.

> **I:** "Hello." (Hold up the **hello** card.)
>
> **I:** "Hello. Yes." (Point to the **hello** card and nod in agreement. Motion for the learners to repeat.)
>
> **G:** "Yes."
>
> **I:** "Fine, thanks." (Hold up the **hello** card again.)
>
> **I:** "Fine, thanks. No." (Point to the **hello** card and shake head in disagreement. Signal for the learners to repeat.)
>
> **G:** "No."

4. Continue with other phrases from Oral Language Activity 1 at random.
5. Repeat phrases as necessary.

Oral Language Activity 2

Introduce Having Polite Interactions

1. Show each card to the group while pronouncing each word slowly and clearly **(Where are you from?, Nice to meet you., Nice to meet you, too., Goodbye.).**
2. Refer to the theme picture, where two individuals are meeting, or other pictures of people meeting and talking, to establish the context for this activity.

> **I:** "Where are you from?" (Hold up the **Where are you from?** card. Motion for the group to repeat together.)
>
> **G:** "Where are you from?"
>
> **I:** "Good. Where are you from?" (Motion for the group to repeat.)
>
> **G:** "Where are you from?"
>
> **I:** "Where are you from?" (Motion for the group to repeat. Put the **Where are you from?** card at the front of the room.)
>
> **G:** "Where are you from?"

3. Introduce the target phrases using the format above.
4. Say each phrase and have the group repeat each one three times.
5. Model for learners how to respond to the question *Where are you from?* with the name of their native country or city or the city or state where they live now.
6. Use the **Mexico** card to introduce the question/response pattern. Then model using the name of learners' current city or state.
7. Prompt each learner to respond with his or her own information.
8. Repeat any phrases more than three times as necessary.

MATERIALS

Large phrase cards (selected cards as specified in activity)

Multiple sets of cards showing responses specified in activity (one set per learner)

Pictures of people meeting and talking

Large map of the world

NOTE

Prior to teaching learners the question *Where are you from?*, practice the names of the learners' countries or cities.

Around the Circle Activity

1. Have the learners form a circle.
2. Post a large map of the world at the front of the room.
3. Introduce each couplet from the dialogue below by modeling and asking the group to listen and repeat each sentence at least three times.

> **I:** "Where are you from?" (Hold up the **Where are you from?** card. Point to a map of the world. Model a response.)
>
> **I:** "Where are you from?" (Motion for the group to repeat.)
>
> **G:** "Where are you from?"
>
> **I:** "Where are you from?" (Point to the map. Motion for the group to repeat.)
>
> **G:** "Where are you from?"
>
> **I:** "Where are you from?" (Motion for the group to repeat.)
>
> **G:** "Where are you from?"

4. Have the learners ask and respond, going around the circle, using the sample dialogue below.

> **Speaker 1:** "Where are you from?"
>
> **Speaker 2:** "Mexico." (Learners should respond with their own information.)
>
> **Speaker 1:** "Nice to meet you."
>
> **Speaker 2:** "Nice to meet you, too."
>
> **Speaker 1:** "Goodbye."
>
> **Speaker 2:** "Goodbye."

5. Ask the learners to use eye contact, gestures, and body language to help them make the target language applicable to real-life situations.
6. Repeat the couplets so that all learners have an opportunity to ask and respond to a full variety of the lines.

Comprehension Check

1. Use the phrases from Oral Language Activity 2 to ask learners at random to respond.
2. Distribute a set of response cards to each learner.

> **I:** "Where are you from?" (Motion to a learner.)
>
> **L:** "Mexico." (Learner should point to Mexico on the map. Alternatively, learner can respond with his or her native country (if different) and point to that on the map.)
>
> **I:** "Nice to meet you." (Motion to a learner for a response.)
>
> **L:** "Nice to meet you, too." (Learner should hold up the **Nice to meet you, too.** card.)
>
> **I:** "Goodbye." (Motion to a learner.)
>
> **L:** "Goodbye." (Learner should hold up the **goodbye** card.)

3. Prompt learners with phrase cards as necessary.
4. Repeat questions at random until the entire group has practiced and shows comprehension of the terms.

Oral Language Activity 3

Review the Pairs

MATERIALS

Large phrase cards (two copies each of **Hello** and **Goodbye** cards)

1. Show each card to the group while pronouncing each word slowly and clearly.
2. Introduce the terms individually, using the format from Oral Language Activity 1 and Oral Language Activity 2.
3. Say each word or phrase and have the group repeat each one three times.
4. Repeat any words or phrases more than three times as necessary.
5. Demonstrate which cards will be paired together for the activity (see matched pairs below).
6. Prompt learners by giving the first phrase in each matched pair and having them respond appropriately with the match.

Matched Pairs

Hello.	Hello.
What's your name?	My name is (Maria).
How are you?	Fine, thanks.
Where are you from?	(Mexico.)
Nice to meet you.	Nice to meet you, too.
Goodbye.	Goodbye.

NOTE

Having one set of phrase cards on one color and the other set on another color will facilitate the learners' matching of pairs. Multiple sets of cards may be used to increase the difficulty of this activity.

Concentration

1. Shuffle the large phrase cards, including both copies of **Hello** and **Goodbye** cards.
2. Spread the cards out on the table facedown so that they are not overlapping.

3. Show learners how to do the activity by turning over two cards.
4. Identify each card or ask the learners to identify the cards.
5. Demonstrate that learners need to match cards according to the pairs presented above.
6. Model getting a matched pair to show how a player with a matched pair keeps the cards and is allowed an extra turn.
7. Model getting two cards that don't match to show how a player with those cards should put them back on the table facedown.
8. Motion for learners to begin the activity by choosing the first person to start.
9. Have each learner choose two cards and identify the phrases.
10. Assist learners as needed.
11. Have learners identify which pairs they collected when the activity is finished.
12. Motion for the learners to hold up the pairs or individual cards to show the group as they identify them.
13. After all cards are collected, count each learner's pairs, and encourage the group to count along.

NOTE

The number of pairs used in this activity may be increased or reduced according to the group's level. The learner who collects the most pairs wins.

Comprehension Check

1. Shuffle the phrase cards (using one copy each of **Hello** and **Goodbye** cards) and place them faceup on the table or other visible surface.
2. Call out a phrase and motion for learners to try to pick up the correct card.
3. Ask the learner who picked up the correct phrase card to repeat the phrase for the group. The learner keeps the card.
4. Continue with the phrases until all of the cards have been collected.
5. Repeat the check as necessary to ensure understanding.

> **I:** "My name is Maria." (Motion for the learners to try to pick up the **My name is Maria** card.)
>
> **L:** "My name is Maria."
>
> **I:** "Good. Hello." (Motion for the learners to try to pick up the **Hello** card.)
>
> **L:** "Hello."

Oral Language Activity 4

NOTE

If appropriate, adjust and vary the name and country in the dialogue, so that learners practice using their own information or names and places that they are familiar with.

Pointing to each word while reading is important to do even if the learners are non-readers or nonliterate.

Introduce the Dialogue

1. Write the sample dialogue (see example below) on the board or on chart paper, and read it for the group, pointing to each word.

Speaker 1: "Hello."
Speaker 2: "Hello."
Speaker 1: "What's your name?"
Speaker 2: "My name is Juan."
Speaker 1: "Where are you from?"
Speaker 2: "Mexico."
Speaker 1: "Nice to meet you."
Speaker 2: "Nice to meet you, too."
Speaker 1: "Goodbye."
Speaker 2: "Goodbye."

---

2. Point to each word whenever the dialogue is repeated in this activity.
3. Introduce paired couplets one by one to help learners master the language of each couplet before putting the whole dialogue together.
4. Say each line of the dialogue and have learners repeat.
5. Build the dialogue gradually, couplet by couplet.
6. Continue adding couplets in sequence to complete one full dialogue.
7. Repeat the entire dialogue as a group three times.
8. Use the large phrase cards to prompt learners as necessary.

Dialogue

1. Write the sample dialogue (see example on the next page) on the board or on chart paper.
2. Practice the dialogue as a group, with the instructor taking the role of Speaker 1 and the group taking the role of Speaker 2, using the written example.
3. Encourage learners to respond with their own information where appropriate.

Speaker 1:	"Hello."
Speaker 2:	"Hello."
Speaker 1:	"What's your name?"
Speaker 2:	"My name is Juan."
Speaker 1:	"Where are you from?"
Speaker 2:	"Mexico."
Speaker 1:	"Nice to meet you."
Speaker 2:	"Nice to meet you, too."
Speaker 1:	"Goodbye."
Speaker 2:	"Goodbye."

4. Help learners answer the questions if they are having trouble.
5. Encourage the use of eye contact, gestures, and body language.
6. Repeat the dialogue, with the instructor and the group switching roles.
7. Continue on to the Comprehension Check when learners can say the dialogue without assistance.

Comprehension Check

1. Hold up two cards and identify one of them correctly.
2. Ask the group to point to the correct card.

> **I:** "Hello." (Hold up the **How are you?** and the **Hello** cards. Motion for the group to respond.)
>
> **G:** "Hello." (Learners should point to the **Hello** card.)

3. Continue with other pairs until all of the phrases have been checked.

Reading Activity

MATERIALS

Large phrase cards

Matching activity sheet (one enlarged and one per learner)

Review

1. Shuffle all of the target phrase cards together.
2. Show each card to the group while pronouncing each word slowly and clearly.
3. Run a finger under each word to help learners begin to recognize the words apart from the pictures.
4. Have the learners repeat the words at least three times.

> **I:** "Goodbye." (Point to the word.)
> **G:** "Goodbye."
> **I:** "Goodbye." (Underline the word with a finger. Motion for the group to repeat the word.)
> **G:** "Goodbye."

5. Continue to review with the cards, using the pattern above.
6. Fold cards in half to show only the words, to help learners become less dependent on the pictures.
7. Move from group to individual practice as learners become more comfortable reading the words without the assistance of the pictures.

Matching Activity

1. Distribute a Matching activity sheet to each learner.
2. Post an enlarged copy of the activity sheet in the front of the room.
3. Place the large phrase cards in a visible location.
4. Demonstrate to learners how to read and match the phrases in Column A correctly to the responses in Column B.
5. On the enlarged activity sheet, point to the first phrase. Prompt learners to read the phrase.
6. Demonstrate looking at the phrases in Column B to find the correct response to match the phrase in column A.
7. Demonstrate how to draw a line between the matching phrases.
8. Motion for learners to draw a line on their own sheets from each phrase in Column A to the corresponding phrase in Column B.
9. Use the large phrase cards to prompt the learners.
10. Assist learners as necessary.

Writing Activity

Review

1. Shuffle all of the target phrase cards together.
2. Show each card to the group while pronouncing each word slowly and clearly.
3. Run a finger under each word to help learners begin to recognize the words apart from the pictures.
4. Have the learners repeat the words at least three times.

> **I:** "Goodbye." (Point to the word.)
>
> **G:** "Goodbye."
>
> **I:** "Goodbye." (Underline the word with a finger. Motion for the group to repeat the word.)
>
> **G:** "Goodbye."

> **NOTE**
>
> Separating words from pictures should be done gradually and after plenty of practice.

5. Continue to review with the cards, using the pattern above.
6. Fold cards in half to show only the words, to help learners become less dependent on the pictures.
7. Move from group to individual practice as learners become more comfortable reading the words and phrases without the assistance of the pictures.

Dialogue Writing Activity

1. Distribute a Dialogue Writing activity sheet to each learner.
2. Post an enlarged copy of the activity sheet in the front of the room.
3. Place the large phrase cards in a visible location.
4. On the enlarged activity sheet, point to the first picture and have learners identify the corresponding phrase.
5. Demonstrate how to write the phrase on the line(s) next to picture.
6. Have learners use the pictures to complete the dialogue.
7. Encourage learners to use the large phrase cards to write the phrases in the dialogue.
8. Assist learners as necessary.
9. Ask learners to perform the dialogue as a group or in pairs after the writing is complete.

Lesson B - Civic Responsibility

Law Enforcement

VOCABULARY

NOUNS
Driver's license
Green card
ID
Immigration officer
Passport
Police officer

VERBS
Answer/Don't answer
Ask
Run/Don't run
Stop
Walk

VERB PHRASE
Ask "Why?"

Objectives
- To help learners understand their rights regarding police questioning
- To help learners avoid situations that might lead to police questioning

Materials Included
- Large reproducible vocabulary cards
- Small reproducible picture cards
- Small reproducible word cards
- Comprehension Check activity sheet
- Talking to a Police Officer activity board
- Name the Pictures activity sheet
- **OK/Not OK** cards (page 250)

Materials Needed
- Die (dice) or coin, to use as a counter
- Small objects to use as place markers (buttons, coins, paper clips, etc.)
- Dice (one die or pair of dice for each learner)
- Alphabet cards (e.g., 3x5 cards with each letter of alphabet written on a single card)

Civics Introduction

Law Enforcement

While both immigration and police officers have the authority to enforce U.S. immigration laws, their authority is limited. It is important that individuals, whether U.S. citizens or not and whether they are documented or not, know their protected rights under the U.S. Constitution.

Until an individual is at the point of being detained, he or she does not have to answer any questions (with the exception of his or her name) asked by an immigration or police officer. If any other question is directed to that individual, he or she does not have to answer. The individual has the right to walk (not run) away, but it is not advisable to walk away from a police or immigration officer. It is better to remain silent or to ask the officer why that officer has stopped the individual. A police officer must have a clear suspicion or specific reason to stop any person, and unless the officer arrests or detains that person, he or she has a Constitutional right not to reply. Similarly, an immigration officer must have "reasonable suspicion, based on specific articulable facts" that an individual is not a U.S. citizen in order to question him or her. The inability to speak English or belonging to a non-dominant ethnic group does not constitute reasonable suspicion.

The above rights apply to an individual who has not already been legally detained by an officer. Once legally detained, the individual must answer the officer's questions. By law, however, the detention must be supported by "reasonable suspicion, based upon specific, articulable facts." If arrested, an individual must be informed of the Miranda rights, that is, the right to remain silent (not to incriminate oneself) until a lawyer is present, the right to be represented by a lawyer, and the right to have a lawyer appointed free of charge if the detained person cannot afford a lawyer.

This topic is important to newly arrived, non-English-speaking adults because their documentation and legal status may be questioned. Awareness of their rights will allow new arrivals to understand when a police or immigration officer is allowed to ask specific questions. They must understand that if they are not yet U.S. citizens, they are required to carry their Permanent Resident card ("green card"), if they are legal residents. If they are U.S. citizens, they are not required to have identification. If stopped while driving, an individual can be asked to show a driver's license (and insurance card), but the officer must articulate a clear reason for stopping the car.

It is important to have learners understand that it is always advisable to speak and behave politely with police or immigration officers, and it could be dangerous to run away (or even to walk away, although that may be within a person's rights). But it is equally important to have learners understand their legal rights.

See Unit 1, "Getting a Lawyer," for information regarding finding legal services and an individual's rights to counsel.

See Unit 3, "Understanding Community Responsibilities," for information on what it means to be a contributing citizen and what an individual's rights are if arrested.

Oral Language Activity 1

MATERIALS

Large noun cards

Comprehension Check activity sheet

Dice

Introduce the Target Nouns

1. Show each noun card to the class while pronouncing each word slowly and clearly.

> **I:** "Police officer." (Motion for the group to repeat together.)
> **G:** "Police officer."
> **I:** "Good. Police officer." (Motion for the group to repeat.)
> **G:** "Police officer."
> **I:** "Police officer." (Motion for the group to repeat. Put the **police officer** card at the front of the room.)
> **G:** "Police officer."

2. Introduce the target nouns (**driver's license, green card, ID, immigration officer, passport,** and **police officer**) using the format above.
3. Say each word and have the group repeat each one three times.
4. Repeat any words more than three times as necessary.

Dice Roll for Nouns

1. Label each large noun card with a number from 1 to 6.
2. Display each card in a visible location.
3. Demonstrate the activity by rolling a die.
4. Count the number on the side facing up and find the card with the corresponding number, as in the example below.
5. Identify verbally the noun with the number corresponding to the number that was rolled with the die.

> **I:** "One, two, three. Three." (Count the number of dots on the side of the die facing up. Point to the card labeled with the number three. Motion for the group to identify it.)
> **G:** "Immigration officer."
> **I:** "Good. Immigration officer."

6. Use one die for the whole group or break a large group into smaller groups and give each group a die.
7. Continue with all members of the group taking turns rolling dice and identifying the cards.
8. Assist learners as necessary.

Comprehension Check Activity

1. Distribute a Comprehension Check activity sheet to each learner.
2. Post an enlarged copy of the activity sheet in the front of the room.

NOTE

Learners will require an ability to count and say numbers, at least 1 through 6, for this activity. Multiple dice and sets of large noun cards may be required for this activity.

3. Motion for the learners to listen carefully with palm open next to an ear.
4. Point to item 1 on the enlarged activity sheet and read the term.

> **I:** "Police officer. Police officer. Which picture? Show me." (Point to each picture in item 1. Motion for a response.)
>
> **G:** "Police officer." (Point to the correct picture in item 1 or say when the instructor is pointing to the correct picture on the enlarged sheet.)
>
> **I:** "Great. OK. Circle it." (On the enlarged activity sheet, show the learners how to draw a circle around the correct picture.)

5. Point to each picture and motion for a response.
6. Continue saying the terms on the Comprehension Check activity sheet. Encourage learners to answer independently.
7. Speak slowly and repeat terms more than once before motioning for the learners to make their selection.
8. Have learners circle the correct picture for each item on their own activity sheets.

Oral Language Activity 2

Introduce the Target Verbs and Verb Phrase

1. Show each verb or verb phrase card to the group while pronouncing each word slowly and clearly.

> **I:** "Stop." (Hold up the **stop** card. Motion for the group to repeat together.)
>
> **G:** "Stop."
>
> **I:** "Good. Stop." (Motion for the group to repeat.)
>
> **G:** "Stop."
>
> **I:** "Stop." (Motion for the group to repeat. Put the **stop** card at the front of the room.)
>
> **G:** "Stop."

2. Introduce the target verbs and the verb phrase, using the format above.
3. Say each word and have the group repeat each one three times.
4. Repeat any words more than three times as necessary.

This activity is primarily intended to reinforce learners' understanding of their rights if stopped by law officers. Although it is within an individual's rights to walk away unless the officer states a specific reason for stopping him or her, it should be made clear to learners that walking away is not the best course of action nowadays. Learners are shown here that **Answer** is not OK, i.e., not required, but they should understand that they have to answer if the officer has an articulated reason for stopping them or if the officer arrests them. If a person is stopped while driving, the officer has the right to ask to see a driver's license.

Sorting Activity

1. Place the **OK** and **Not OK** cards on the board or other visible surface to create two column headings.
2. Review verb cards for the group, associating each one with OK or Not OK (see correct placement below).
3. Place the cards under the appropriate heading of OK or Not OK.

> **I:** "Don't answer." (Hold up the **don't answer** card and motion for the group to repeat.)
>
> **G:** "Don't answer."
>
> **I:** "Don't answer. OK." (Hold up the **don't answer** card. Motion for the group to repeat.)
>
> **G:** "Don't answer." (Place the **don't answer** card in the OK column.)

4. Continue reviewing each card and showing the group how to place them in the correct columns.

Correct placement

Ask "Why?" = OK	Don't run = OK
Don't answer = OK	Walk = OK
Answer = Not OK	Ask passport = Not OK
Ask driver's license = Not OK	Run = Not OK
Ask green card = Not OK	Stop = Not OK
Ask ID = Not OK	

5. After each placement has been modeled and is understood by the learners, practice the sorting activity with the group.
6. Take the verb cards and reshuffle them.
7. Hold up each card and have learners identify the correct column in which it belongs.
8. Repeat the sorting activity as necessary to help ensure understanding.

Comprehension Check

1. Shuffle the verb cards and distribute them to the learners at random.
2. Keep the **OK** and **Not OK** cards posted as column headings.
3. Call out the verbs in random order.
4. Ask the learner with the corresponding card to hold it up when it is called by the instructor.
5. Have learners place the cards under the heading OK or Not OK.
6. Assist the learners as necessary.

Oral Language Activity 3

MATERIALS

Large verb cards

Small verb picture cards
(two sets)

OK/Not OK cards

NOTE

Having one set of verb cards on one color and the other set on another color will facilitate the learners' matching of pairs.

NOTE

Make sure learners also understand the exceptions to these situations, namely, that an individual has to answer if a police officer states a reasonable suspicion and that police can ask for a driver's license if a driver is stopped and given a reason for the stop.

Introduce Situations Concentration

1. Introduce situations that could result in police questioning.

Situations

Answer = Not OK	Ask passport = Not OK
Ask driver's license = Not OK	Ask "Why?" = OK
Ask green card = Not OK	Run = Not OK
Ask ID = Not OK	Stop = Not OK

2. Make sure the group understands the terms before starting the situations concentration activity.

Situations Concentration

1. Shuffle two sets of small verb picture cards.
2. Spread cards out on the table facedown and arrange them so that they are not overlapping.
3. Show learners how to do the activity by turning over two cards.
4. Model getting a matched pair to show how a player with a matched pair keeps the cards and is allowed an extra turn.
5. Model getting cards that do not match to show how the player should put the cards back on the table, facedown.
6. Ask the learners who have found pairs to say *Not OK* to reinforce the concept that the behavior is not legally required or is not advisable for learners and may not be legal (under most conditions) for police officers.

> **I:** "Answer." (Turn one card over. Motion for the group to repeat.)
> **G:** "Answer."
> **I:** "Answer." (Turn another card over. Motion for the group to repeat.)
> **I:** "Answer. Not OK." (Motion for the group to repeat.)
> **G:** "Not OK."
> **I:** "Answer." (Turn one card over. Motion for the group to repeat.)
> **G:** "Answer."
> **I:** "Stop." (Turn one card over. Motion for the group to repeat.)
> **G:** "Stop."
> **I:** "Stop. Not OK." (Motion for the group to repeat.)
> **G:** "Not OK."

7. Continue the activity until all of the pairs have been collected and identified.
8. Count each learner's pairs (and encourage the group to count along).

Comprehension Check

1. Hold up two cards, one that displays a behavior that is OK and one that is Not OK.
2. Ask the group to say and point to the OK or the Not OK behavior, depending on which is asked for.
3. Make sure learners understand that both cards may show OK or Not OK behaviors.

> **I:** "Which is OK?" (Hold up the **run** and **walk** cards. Motion for the group to respond.)
>
> **G:** "Walk." (Point to the **walk** card.)
>
> **I:** "Which is Not OK?" (Hold up the **answer** and **stop** cards. Motion for a response.)
>
> **G:** "Answer. Stop." (Point to the **answer** and **stop** cards.)

Oral Language Activity 4

Introduce the Talking to a Police Officer Activity

1. Place the Talking to a Police Officer activity board on a table or other surface accessible to learners.
2. Point to each picture on the activity board and have learners identify it.
3. If necessary, identify the picture and have learners repeat the term.
4. Distribute one place marker to each learner.
5. Roll a die or flip a coin to model the activity.
6. Count the number of spaces to move the place marker on the board.
7. Model the activity by moving the appropriate number of spaces.

Talking to a Police Officer Activity

1. Have learners take turns rolling dice or flipping a coin and moving around the board.
2. Motion for learners to identify the pictures on the activity board where the place marker lands.
3. Have learners indicate which scenario is OK or Not OK.

Scenarios

OK	NOT OK
Don't answer	Answer
Don't run	Ask for driver's license
Walk	Ask for green card
Ask "Why?"	Ask for ID
	Ask for passport
	Run
	Stop

4. Assist learners as necessary.

Comprehension Check

1. Pass out **Yes/No** cards to each learner.
2. Hold up a vocabulary card and say what it is.
3. Motion for the learners to hold up their **Yes** cards.

> **I:** "ID." (Hold up the **ID** card. Motion for a response.)
>
> **I:** "ID. Yes." (Hold up the **Yes** card. Motion for the group to repeat.)
>
> **G:** "Yes." (Hold up the **Yes** card.)

4. Use the pattern above to introduce how to use the **No** card.

> **I:** "Stop." (Hold up the **ID** card. Motion for a response.)
>
> **I:** "Stop. No." (Hold up the **No** card. Motion for the group to repeat.)
>
> **G:** "No." (Hold up the **No** card.)

5. Review all of the noun and verb cards, identifying cards correctly or incorrectly at random, to check learner's understanding.

Reading Activity

MATERIALS

Large noun cards

Large verb cards

Instructor-made alphabet cards

Review

1. Shuffle all of the target noun and verb cards together.
2. Show each card to the group while pronouncing each word slowly and clearly.
3. Run a finger under each word to help learners begin to recognize the words apart from the pictures.
4. Have the learners repeat the words at least three times.

> **I:** "Police officer." (Point to the words.)
>
> **G:** "Police officer."
>
> **I:** "Police officer." (Underline the words with a finger. Motion for the group to repeat the words.)
>
> **G:** "Police officer."

5. Continue to review with the cards, using the pattern above.
6. Fold cards in half to show only the words, to help learners become less dependent on the pictures.
7. Move from group to individual practice as learners become more comfortable reading the words without the assistance of the pictures.

Guess the Word Activity

1. Use the target nouns and verbs from this lesson.
2. On the board or on chart paper, draw short horizontal lines to represent each letter in one of the words.
3. Draw a stick figure of a person next to the letter blanks.
4. Pass out alphabet cards in random order, so that each learner has more than one card.
5. Divide the class into teams.
6. Motion for the learners to make guesses one at a time about the missing letters, using the alphabet cards.
7. Encourage the learners to hold up the cards and identify them as a guess is made.
8. Write each correct letter that a learner guesses on the appropriate line.
9. Write any incorrect letter in a separate location on the board or chart paper. Then erase one of the stick figure's body parts (hand, foot, leg, arm, head, etc.).
10. Give all of the learners a chance to guess letters.
11. Have learners read the word out loud once all the letters have been filled in.

Writing Activity

MATERIALS

Large noun cards

Large verb cards

Name the Pictures activity sheet (one enlarged and one per learner)

Review

1. Shuffle all of the target noun and verb cards together.
2. Show each card to the group while pronouncing each word slowly and clearly.
3. Run a finger under each word to help learners begin to recognize the words apart from the pictures.
4. Have the learners repeat the words at least three times.

> **I:** "Run." (Point to the word.)
> **G:** "Run."
> **I:** "Run." (Underline the word with a finger. Motion for the group to repeat the word.)
> **G:** "Run."

5. Continue to review with the cards, using the pattern above.
6. Fold cards in half to show only the words, to help learners become less dependent on the pictures.
7. Move from group to individual practice as learners become more comfortable reading the words without the assistance of the pictures.

Name the Pictures Activity

1. Distribute a Name the Pictures activity sheet to each learner.
2. Display the large vocabulary cards in a visible location.
3. Post an enlarged copy of the activity sheet in the front of the room.
4. On the enlarged sheet, demonstrate how to match a word to its corresponding picture by drawing a line between them.
5. Model writing the correct word on the line provided.
6. Have learners identify each picture and read each word on the activity sheet.
7. Have learners complete their own activity sheets by matching all of the pictures with words and writing them in the spaces provided.
8. Encourage learners to refer to the displayed vocabulary cards to write the words.
9. Assist learners as necessary.

Unit Review Activity

MATERIALS

Unit Review activity sheet (one enlarged and one per learner)

Large vocabulary cards (from Lessons A & B)

NOTE

The Unit Review Activity can be done as a group activity for reinforcing the concepts learned in the lesson or done as an individual activity for assessment purposes.

OK or Not OK Review Activity

1. Use large vocabulary cards from Lessons A and B to review the vocabulary and concepts of the unit.
2. Post an enlarged copy of the activity sheet in the front of the room or in another visible location.
3. Point to each picture on the enlarged activity sheet and ask learners to identify it. Help learners understand that the pictures in each item show situations that might arise in dealing with a police officer, shown in the picture above the line.
4. Distribute a copy of the Unit Review Activity sheet to each learner.
5. On the enlarged activity sheet, point to the picture or set of pictures in each item. Elicit from learners whether the action represented by the combination or individual picture in the item is OK (desirable, legal, or an appropriate action) or Not OK (not desirable, illegal, or an unwise action).
6. Ask learners to complete the activity on their own sheets. If necessary, use the enlarged activity sheet to model for learners how to check the correct column to indicate that the item is OK or Not OK.

Unit 2 *Communicating with Neighbors and the Police* Lesson A *Life Skill*

Central Theme Picture

Hello.

Goodbye.

Fine,
thanks.

How are
you?

Nice to meet you.

Nice to meet you, too.

My name is Maria.

What's your name?

Where are you from?

Mexico.

Unit 2 Lesson A *Life Skill*   Small Picture Cards

Unit 2 Lesson A *Life Skill*   Small Picture Cards

How are you today?

Unit 2 Lesson A *Life Skill*   Small Picture Cards

Fine, thanks.

Unit 2 Lesson A *Life Skill*   Small Picture Cards

Nice to meet you.

Unit 2 Lesson A *Life Skill*   Small Picture Cards

Nice to meet you, too.

Unit 2 Lesson A *Life Skill*   Small Picture Cards

Unit 2 Lesson A *Life Skill*   Small Picture Cards

Unit 2 Lesson A *Life Skill*   Small Picture Cards

Unit 2 Lesson A *Life Skill*   Small Picture Cards

Unit 2 Lesson A *Life Skill*   Small Picture Cards

Hello.

Goodbye.

How are you?

Fine, thanks.

Nice to meet you.

Nice to meet you, too.

What's your name?

My name is <u>Maria</u>.

Where are you from?

Mexico.

Matching Activity

Look at the phrases in Column A. Draw a line to the matching phrase in Column B.

Column A

How are you?

What's your name?

Where are you from?

Nice to meet you.

Column B

Mexico.

Nice to meet you, too.

My name is <u>Maria</u>.

Fine, thanks.

Dialogue Writing Activity

Look at the pictures. Write the word(s). Complete the dialogue.

1.  _____.

   Hello.

2.  _____ _____ _____?

3. **My name is** _____.

4.  _____ _____ _____ _____?

5. _____.

6. **Nice** _____ **meet** _____.

7.  _____ _____ _____ _____, _____.

PERMANENT RESIDENT CARD

NAME PADILLA GOMEZ, JUAN CARLOS

INS A# 123-456-789

Birthdate   Category   Sex
12/15/67   M

Country
Mexico

Resident Since: 11/03/09
02/18/93

C1USA0123456789ABC987654321<<
1234567A987654MEX<<<<<<<<<5
PADILLA GOMEZ<<JUAN CARLOS<<<<

Green card

✂

STATE DRIVER'S LICENSE

Commissioner of Motor Vehicles

Joe Commissioner

ID: 012 345 678

DOB: 12-15-67

DRIVER LICENSE

JUAN CARLOS PADILLA GOMEZ
PO BOX 123
ANYTOWN   NY
12345

SEX: M   EYES: BR   HT: 6-1   CLASS: D

ISSUED: 12-15-05   EXPIRES: 12-15-13

Juan Carlos Padilla Gomez   8005456548

Driver's license

ID

Immigration officer

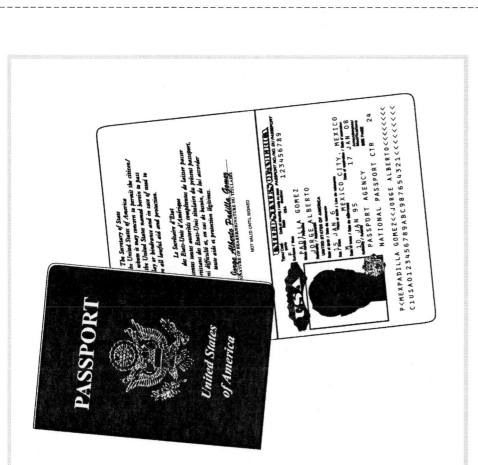

Police
officer

✂

Passport

Answer

Don't answer

Don't run

✂

Run

Stop

Walk

Yes

No

Ask

Ask "Why?"

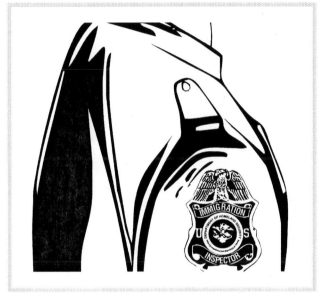

Unit 2 Lesson B *Civic Responsibility*   Small Picture Cards

Unit 2 Lesson B *Civic Responsibility*   Small Picture Cards

Unit 2 Lesson B *Civic Responsibility*   Small Picture Cards

Unit 2 Lesson B *Civic Responsibility*   Small Picture Cards

Unit 2 Lesson B *Civic Responsibility*   Small Picture Cards

Unit 2 Lesson B *Civic Responsibility*   Small Picture Cards

Unit 2 Lesson B *Civic Responsibility*   Small Picture Cards

Unit 2 Lesson B *Civic Responsibility*   Small Picture Cards

Unit 2 Lesson B *Civic Responsibility*   Small Picture Cards

Unit 2 Lesson B *Civic Responsibility*   Small Picture Cards

Unit 2 Lesson B *Civic Responsibility*   Small Picture Cards

Unit 2 Lesson B *Civic Responsibility*   Small Picture Cards

Unit 2 Lesson B *Civic Responsibility*　　　Small Picture Cards

Ask

Unit 2 Lesson B *Civic Responsibility*　　　Small Word Cards

Unit 2 Lesson B *Civic Responsibility*　　　Small Picture Cards

Ask
"Why?"

Unit 2 Lesson B *Civic Responsibility*　　　Small Word Cards

Driver's license

Green card

ID

Immigration officer

Passport

Police officer

Answer

Don't answer

Run

Don't run

Stop

Walk

Comprehension Check Activity

Listen. Circle the correct picture.

<u>Teacher reads:</u>

1. Police officer

2. Passport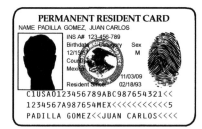

3. Driver's license

4. Green card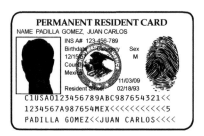

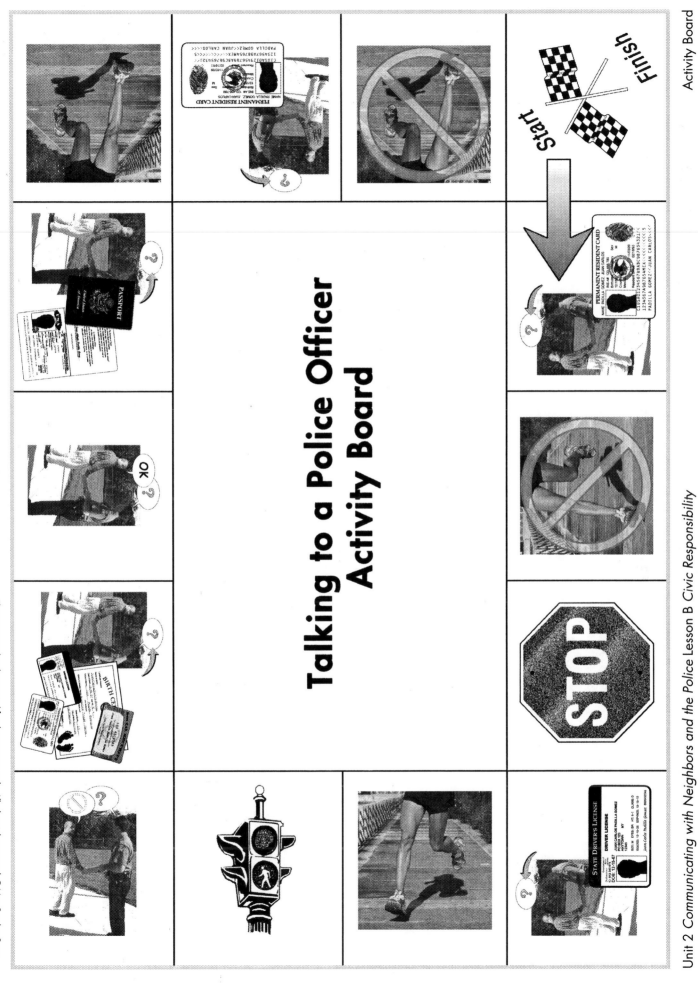

Talking to a Police Officer
Activity Board

Unit 2 Communicating with Neighbors and the Police Lesson B Civic Responsibility

Activity Board

Name the Pictures Activity

Look at the pictures. Write the word(s).

Immigration officer

Passport

ID

Police officer

Green card

Driver's license

1.

_____

2. _____

_____

3.

_____

4. _____

5. _____

_____

6.

_____

Check OK or Not OK for each picture or set of pictures.

	OK	Not OK
1.	___	___
2.	___	___
3.	___	___
4.	___	___
5.	___	___
6.	___	___

Unit 2 *Communicating with Neighbors and the Police*

Unit Review

Unit 3

Understanding Community Responsibilities

Your Responsibilities

VOCABULARY

NOUNS

Citizens

Family

Law

People

Police officer

Property

Rule

School

VERBS

Help

Obey

Respect

Objective

Learners will understand and be able to state basic behaviors of a citizen: to obey rules, laws, and the police; to respect property; and to help others

Materials Included

- Central theme picture
- Large reproducible vocabulary cards
- Bingo boards
- Sentence/Picture Matching activity sheet
- Complete the Sentences activity sheet
- **Yes/No** cards

Materials Needed

- Additional instructor copy (enlarged) of the activity sheets
- Family photographs or pictures showing families
- Law book(s)
- Pictures of personal property, such as a house or a car
- Pictures of police officers, men, women, and children
- Pictures of school(s) and various workplaces
- Pictures or instructor-made replicas of signs regulating behavior *(no cell phone, keep off grass, no parking, etc.)*
- Pictures for teaching verbs, showing someone obeying a teacher, police officer, or other person of authority; someone helping another person (e.g., the **help** card from Unit 1, page 50); and someone handling personal belongings with care or showing respect to another person, such as a parent or grandparent, police officer, or clergy
- Small objects (scraps of paper, coins, paper clips, etc.) to use as Bingo board markers

Central Theme Picture

MATERIALS

Theme picture

Introduce the Theme Picture

1. Show learners the theme picture and ask for a response.
2. Encourage learners to say anything about the picture that they can.

> **I:** "What's happening in this picture?" (Point out key things about the picture to elicit a response.)

POSSIBLE RESPONSES

Man

Neighbor

People

Street

Tree

Woman

Oral Language Activity 1

MATERIALS

Large noun cards

Family photographs or pictures showing families

Law book(s)

Pictures of personal property, such as a house or a car

Pictures of police officers, men, women and children

Pictures of school(s) and various workplaces

Pictures or instructor-made replicas of signs regulating behavior (no cell phone, keep off grass, no parking, etc.)

Bingo boards and Bingo board markers

Yes/No cards (one set per learner)

Introduce the Target Nouns

1. Show each large noun card to the group while pronouncing the words slowly and clearly.

> **I:** "Citizens." (Hold up the **citizens** card. Motion for the learners to repeat.)
> **G:** "Citizens."
> **I:** "Good. Citizens." (Motion for learners to repeat.)
> **G:** "Citizens."
> **I:** "Very good. What's this?" (Hold up the **citizens** card. Motion for a response.)
> **G:** "Citizens."

2. Introduce the other target nouns using the format above (**family, law, people, police officer, property, rule,** and **school**).
3. Use mime, pictures, and realia as necessary to help the group understand the target nouns.
4. Say each word and have the group repeat each one three times.
5. Repeat any words more than three times as necessary.

Bingo Activity

1. Distribute one Bingo board and a set of Bingo board markers to each learner.
2. Show learners that, to win, a player must mark five squares in a row (horizontally, vertically, or diagonally).
3. Mix up the large noun cards and place them in a basket, box, or envelope so learners can easily choose them.

4. Ask learners to identify each vocabulary word when they choose a card.
5. Have learners repeat each word as the boards are marked.
6. Draw a card and show it to the group, motioning for the learners to respond.

> **I:** "What's this?" (Hold up the **family** card. Motion for a response.)
>
> **G:** "Family."
>
> **I:** "Great. Family." (Show learners how to find the family picture on their boards and how to mark it. Motion for the group to repeat the word.)
>
> **G:** "Family."

NOTE

Five marked boxes in a row horizontally, vertically, or diagonally = Bingo.

7. Continue the activity until a learner has five squares in a row marked.
8. Assist learners as necessary.
9. Have learners call out *Bingo* when they have five squares in a row marked (horizontally, vertically, or diagonally).

Comprehension Check

1. Distribute **Yes/No** cards to each learner.
2. Hold up vocabulary cards one by one. Identify cards correctly and incorrectly at random.
3. Ask learners to hold up the **Yes** card when a term is correctly identified and the **No** card when the term is incorrectly identified.
4. Model the activity for learners.
5. Repeat the check as necessary, varying the identification of words, to help ensure that the terms are understood by the group.

Oral Language Activity 2

Introduce the Target Verbs

1. Introduce the target verbs using gestures and realia, as in the suggestions on the next page, to demonstrate the meaning of the verbs. Use pictures to clarify meaning.

MATERIALS

Large noun cards

Pictures showing someone obeying a teacher, police officer, or other person of authority; someone helping another person; and someone handling personal belongings with care or showing respect to another person, such as a parent or grandparent, police officer, or clergy

Suggestions for introducing verbs

Obey - act out following directions of a teacher, parent, or police officer; play "Simon says" to illustrate the concept of **obey**

Help - demonstrate doing something for another person or giving assistance, such as carrying a heavy box; ask a student for assistance in doing something

Respect - show giving respect to others' belongings by using something and returning it carefully; mime acting respectfully to an older person or an official

2. Say the terms for learners, pronouncing each one slowly and clearly.

> **I:** "Obey." (Use mime and realia as suggested above to demonstrate the verb obey. Motion for the learners to repeat.)
>
> **G:** "Obey."
>
> **I:** "Good. Obey." (Motion for learners to repeat.)
>
> **G:** "Obey."
>
> **I:** "Very good. Obey." (Motion for learners to repeat.)
>
> **G:** "Obey."

3. Introduce **help** and **respect** using the format above.

Identify the Verb Activity

1. Demonstrate each verb and have the learners identify each one.
2. Ask learners to associate magazine pictures or realia with each verb.
3. Have the learners demonstrate the verbs and use the pictures or realia as a reference.

Suggestions for Demonstration and Realia

Obey - show following directions of a teacher, parent, or police officer using magazine pictures and/or gestures or mime

Help - demonstrate doing something for another person or giving assistance; ask a learner for assistance in doing something

Respect - show giving respect to others' belongings using real objects (anything in the classroom) or magazine pictures; show acting respectfully to an older person or official

4. Have learners verbally identify each verb as it is demonstrated.

Comprehension Check

1. Place a picture of a parent, teacher, boss, or police officer on the board or on chart paper and associate it with the verb **obey.**
2. Put a picture of someone helping another in a visible location and associate it with the verb **help.**

3. Attach a picture of a person taking care of an object or showing respect to another person and associate this picture with the term **respect.**
4. Remove these three pictures from the board and place them on a table or other available surface.
5. Have the group form a circle around the pictures.
6. Call out each verb and ask the group to point to the picture that represents that term.
7. Repeat as necessary to help ensure that the group has a solid understanding of the verbs **obey, help,** and **respect.**

Oral Language Activity 3

Review of Target Vocabulary

1. Review the vocabulary from Oral Language Activity 1 and Oral Language Activity 2 by showing each noun card or demonstrating each verb and motioning for a response.

> **I:** "What's this?" (Hold up the **law** card. Motion for a response.)
>
> **G:** "Law."
>
> **I:** "Good. Law." (Hold up the **law** card.)

2. State the correct term and gesture for the group to repeat the word when learners need additional assistance or verbal practice.
3. Introduce all of the vocabulary terms, repeating them as necessary.
4. Assist learners as needed.

Create Sentences Activity

1. Hold up the **citizens** card and ask learners to identify the word verbally.
2. Place the **citizens** card at the front of the room.
3. Hold up each additional card (suggested on the next page), along with pictures representing each verb and have the learners identify the terms.
4. Use the examples in the suggestions on the next page to guide the combinations of cards and pictures.

Suggestions for Making Sentences

<u>Citizens:</u>

Respect/property = Citizens respect property.

Obey/rules/laws = Citizens obey rules and laws.

Help/people = Citizens help people.

5. Make sentences using the cards and pictures.
6. First point to individual cards or pictures and say the words individually. Gradually blend them into a sentence.
7. Have the group repeat each one at least three times.

> **I:** "Citizens. Respect. Property." (Point to each card or picture and ask the group to repeat.)
>
> **G:** "Citizens. Respect. Property."
>
> **I:** "Citizens respect property." (Motion for the group to repeat.)
>
> **G:** "Citizens respect property."

8. Continue with other combinations of cards and pictures to make sentences.
9. Assist learners as necessary.

Comprehension Check

1. Place all of the cards and pictures used in Oral Language Activity 3 faceup on a table or other available surface.
2. Call out sentences and ask the group to point in order to the picture and cards representing each sentence as it is called.

> **I:** "Citizens help people." (Motion for the group to point to each picture and card.)
>
> **G:** "Citizens help people." (Learners should point to the **citizens**, **help**, and **people** corresponding cards and picture.)

3. Continue with other sentences to help ensure the group's comprehension.
4. Repeat sentences at random for sufficient verbal practice.

Oral Language Activity 4

Introduce the Dialogue

1. Write the sample dialogue (see example on the next page) on the board or on chart paper.

MATERIALS

Large vocabulary cards

Pictures representing target vocabulary

NOTE

Pointing to the words while reading is important to do even if the learners are non-readers or nonliterate.

Use the suggestions in Oral Language Activity 2 for demonstrating the verbs.

In this dialogue, learners are instructed that good citizens obey the police. See Unit 2 for an exception to this rule.

2. Read each line for the group slowly, running a finger under each word as the line is read aloud.

Speaker 1:	"What should citizens do?" (Hold up the **people** card. Hold up a picture of someone helping another. Demonstrate helping another person. Motion for a response.)
Speaker 2:	"Help people."
Speaker 1:	"What should citizens do?" (Hold up the **police officer** card and demonstrate obeying a police officer. Motion for a response.)
Speaker 2:	"Obey police officers."
Speaker 1:	"What should citizens do?" (Hold up the **rule** and **law** cards. Demonstrate the verb **obey** by associating it with obeying rules (such as *No smoking*) and laws. Motion for a response.)
Speaker 2:	"Obey rules and laws."
Speaker 1:	"What should citizens do?" (Hold up an individual's belongings and the **property** card. Mime showing respect for property. Motion for a response.)
Speaker 2:	"Respect property."

3. Introduce the dialogue, taking the role of Speaker 1 and asking the learners to respond as Speaker 2.
4. Repeat the dialogue as a group three times.
5. Use pictures to clarify meaning and reinforce the prompts.

Dialogue Activity

1. Write the sample dialogue (see example below) on the board or on chart paper. Point to each word as you read the dialogue to the group.
2. Point to each word whenever the dialogue is repeated in this activity.

Speaker 1:	"What should citizens do?" (Hold up the **people** card. Hold up a picture of someone helping another. Demonstrate helping another person. Motion for a response.)
Speaker 2:	"Help people."
Speaker 1:	"What should citizens do?" (Hold up the **police officer** card and demonstrate obeying police. Motion for a response.)
Speaker 2:	"Obey police officers."
Speaker 1:	"What should citizens do?" (Hold up the **rule** and **law** cards. Demonstrate the verb **obey** and associate with rules and laws. Motion for a response.)
Speaker 2:	"Obey rules and laws."
Speaker 1:	"What should citizens do?" (Hold up someone's belonging and the **property** card. Demonstrate showing respect for property. Motion for a response.)
Speaker 2:	"Respect property."

3. Perform the dialogue as a group three times, with the instructor taking the role of Speaker 1 and the learners responding as Speaker 2.
4. Use the vocabulary cards, pictures representing target vocabulary, and mime or gestures to illustrate the dialogue.
5. Assist learners as necessary.

Comprehension Check

1. Place pictures that represent **obey, respect,** and **help** in a visible location.
2. Call out the nouns and noun combinations practiced in Oral Language Activity 4.
3. Have the group point to the picture corresponding to the appropriate verb for each noun or noun combination to check learners' understanding of the verb + noun combinations practiced in the dialogue.
4. Model the activity for learners.

> **I:** "Rules and laws." (Point to the **obey** picture. Motion for the group to point to the **obey** picture.)
> **G:** "Obey." (Learners should point to the **obey** picture.)
> **I:** "Property." (Motion for a response.)
> **G:** "Respect." (Learners should point to the **respect** picture.)

5. Continue calling out different nouns and noun combinations and asking the group to point to the corresponding verb pictures.
6. Repeat as necessary to help ensure the group's comprehension of the verb + noun associations.

Reading Activity

MATERIALS

Large noun cards

Sentence/Picture Matching activity sheet (one enlarged and one per learner)

Review

1. Shuffle all of the target vocabulary cards.
2. Show each card to the group while pronouncing each word slowly and clearly.
3. Run a finger under each word to help learners begin to recognize the words apart from the pictures.
4. Have the learners repeat the words at least three times.

> **I:** "Police officer." (Point to the words.)
> **G:** "Police officer."
> **I:** "Police officer." (Underline the words with a finger. Motion for the group to repeat the words.)
> **G:** "Police officer."

5. Continue to review with the cards, using the pattern on the previous page.
6. Fold cards in half to show only the words, to help learners become less dependent on the pictures.
7. Move from group to individual practice as learners become more comfortable reading the words without the assistance of the pictures.

Sentence/Picture Matching Activity

1. Distribute a Sentence/Picture Matching activity sheet to each learner.
2. Post an enlarged activity sheet at the front of the room and place the large vocabulary cards in a visible location to assist the group.
3. On the enlarged activity sheet, point to each sentence and ask the learners to identify each word in the sentence. If necessary, say the sentence and have learners repeat.
4. Point to the sets of pictures on the enlarged activity sheet. Point to each picture in the sets and have learners identify each one.
5. Demonstrate for learners how to draw a line from the sentence to the corresponding set of pictures.
6. Ask the group to match sentences and pictures on their own activity sheets.
7. Assist learners as necessary.

Writing Activity

Review

1. Shuffle all of the target vocabulary cards.
2. Show each card to the group while pronouncing each word slowly and clearly.
3. Run a finger under each word to help learners begin to recognize the words apart from the pictures.
4. Have the learners repeat the words at least three times.

> **I:** "School." (Point to the word.)
> **G:** "School."
> **I:** "School." (Underline the word with a finger. Motion for the group to repeat the word.)
> **G:** "School."

5. Continue to review with the cards, using the pattern above.
6. Fold cards in half to show only the words, to help learners

become less dependent on the pictures.

7. Move from group to individual practice as learners become more comfortable reading the words without the assistance of the pictures.

Complete the Sentences Activity

1. Distribute a Complete the Sentences activity sheet to each learner.
2. Post an enlarged activity sheet at the front of the room and place the large vocabulary cards in a visible location to assist the group.
3. On the enlarged activity sheet, point to the pictures in each item and have learners identify them.
4. Have the group identify the missing words in each sentence. On the enlarged activity sheet, model writing the missing words on the lines provided.
5. Have learners write the missing words to complete the sentences on their own activity sheets.
6. Assist learners as necessary.

Your Rights If Arrested

VOCABULARY

NOUNS
Court

Lawyer

Questions

ADJECTIVE
Free

VERBS
Arrest

Ask

Stop

Talk

ADVERB
On time

Objective
Learners will be able to state what they should do if they are arrested by the police

Materials Included
- Large reproducible vocabulary cards
- Find the Word activity sheet
- Fill in the Missing Words activity sheet
- **Yes/No** cards
- **OK/Not OK** cards (page 250)

Materials Needed
- Additional instructor copy (enlarged) of the activity sheets
- Long piece of card stock or other instructor-devised method to use as a tapper (one for each learner)
- A pair of toy handcuffs
- Pictures of stop signs and people talking
- Picture representing **obey** from Lesson A
- Real clock or instructor-made mock-up of a clock; pictures of clocks showing various times

Civics Introduction

Your Rights If Arrested

To uphold the standards of a society, citizens must obey rules, laws, and the police. They also should respect property and help others. These responsibilities are important for maintaining order and for protecting people's rights and lives. By participating in society as a good citizen, an individual can contribute to the well-being of the society in which he or she lives.

If an individual breaks the law, the U.S. legal system assumes that an individual is innocent until proven guilty. Law enforcement officers must abide by the laws that protect all citizens, even during arrest. The reading of the Miranda rights provides individuals who are suspected of a crime the right not to speak with the police until they have a lawyer present, the right to hire a lawyer to represent them, or the right to have a lawyer appointed free of charge if they cannot afford one. The reading of the Miranda rights should be conducted by a police officer and be understood by the accused.

This topic is important to newly arrived, non-English-speaking adults because they need to know the laws of their new community, which may be different from those of their native country. New arrivals should be aware of their rights in the U.S., including Miranda rights and other rights if they are arrested. To participate fully and actively in their new community, they should clearly understand what is expected of them as new members of society.

Oral Language Activity 1

MATERIALS

Large noun cards (from Lessons A & B; two sets)

Large adjective card

Long piece of card stock or other instructor-devised method to use as a tapper (one per learner)

Introduce the Target Nouns and Adjective

1. Hold up each noun card and pronounce each word slowly and clearly.
2. Ask the group to repeat each noun at least three times.

> **I:** "Court." (Hold up the **court** card. Motion for learners to repeat.)
>
> **G:** "Court."
>
> **I:** "Good. Court." (Motion for learners to repeat.)
>
> **G:** "Court."
>
> **I:** "Very good. What's this?" (Hold up the **court** card. Motion for a response.)
>
> **G:** "Court."

3. Introduce the other target nouns (**court, lawyer,** and **questions**).
4. Introduce the adjective **free** using the same method.
5. Use mime and gestures as necessary to help the group understand each term.
6. Review nouns from Lesson A to prepare for including them in the Tap Activity.
7. Continue on to the Tap Activity when the learners understand and can identify each noun.

Tap Activity

1. Place one set of the target nouns (from Lessons A & B) and the target adjective faceup on the table or other available surface so that each card is visible to the group.
2. Pass out tappers (one for each learner).
3. Motion for the learners to listen carefully by holding one hand up to an ear with palm open.
4. Hold up a card from the second set and identify it verbally.
5. Look for the corresponding card on the table and identify it with the tapper.
6. Motion for the learners to hold up their tappers to begin.

> **I:** "Ready?" (Hold the tapper up.)
>
> **G:** "OK."
>
> **I:** "Questions." (Hold up the **questions** card and identify it verbally. Motion for the learners to try to quickly identify the corresponding card and tap it.)

7. Ask the learner whose tapper identifies the correct card first to pick the card up and repeat the word it represents.
8. Have the learner identify which cards he or she holds when all of the cards have been collected.

Comprehension Check

1. Hold up each target noun card or adjective card for the group.
2. Introduce the cards one by one, identifying them correctly and incorrectly at random.
3. Model how to say Yes when the card is correctly identified, and No when it is incorrectly identified.

> **I:** "Court." (Hold up the **court** card.)
>
> **I:** "Court. Yes." (Point to the **court** card and nod in agreement. Motion for the learners to repeat.)
>
> **G:** "Yes."
>
> **I:** "Lawyer." (Hold up the **court** card again.)
>
> **I:** "Lawyer. No." (Point to the **court** card and gesture disagreement. Motion for the learners to repeat.)
>
> **G:** "No."

4. Continue with other cards at random.
5. Repeat words as necessary.

Oral Language Activity 2

MATERIALS

Large verb and adverb cards

A pair of toy handcuffs

Pictures of stop signs and people talking

Real or mock-up of a clock and pictures of clocks

Introduce the Target Verbs and Adverb

1. Show each large vocabulary card to the group while pronouncing each word slowly and clearly.

> **I:** "Arrest." (Hold up the **arrest** card. Motion for the learners to repeat.)
>
> **G:** "Arrest."
>
> **I:** "Good. Arrest." (Motion for learners to repeat together.)
>
> **G:** "Arrest."
>
> **I:** "Very good. What's this?" (Hold up the **arrest** card. Motion for a response.)
>
> **G:** "Arrest."

2. Introduce each of the target terms using the format above (**arrest, ask, stop, talk,** and **on time**).
3. Use mime and realia or pictures as necessary to help the group understand the target verbs.

Demonstrate the Verbs and Adverb Activity

1. Hold up one of the verb cards and motion for the learners to respond.

> **I:** "What's this?" (Hold up the **arrest** card. Motion for learners to respond.)
>
> **G:** "Arrest."

2. Put the card down and model the action of **arrest** using toy handcuffs.
3. Introduce all of the verb and adverb cards and model each action, using pictures or realia as necessary. Show various times with the clock or pictures of clocks to demonstrate **on time.**
4. Identify each term orally and have the group repeat each one at least three times.
5. Show each card and ask the group to mime or demonstrate the term and then identify it verbally.
6. Continue on to the Comprehension Check when learners can identify each term without assistance.

Comprehension Check

1. Place all of the target verb and adverb cards faceup on the table or other available surface.
2. Call out each term and ask the group to repeat and point to the correct card.

> **I:** "Arrest." (Motion for a response.)
>
> **G:** "Arrest." (Learners should point to the **arrest** card.)

Oral Language Activity 3

Review the Target Vocabulary

1. Review the vocabulary from Oral Language Activities 1 and 2 by showing the cards and motioning for a response.

> **I:** "What's this?" (Hold up the **lawyer** card. Motion for a response.)
>
> **G:** "Lawyer."
>
> **I:** "Good. Lawyer." (Hold up the **lawyer** card.)

2. If necessary, say the correct words as needed and gesture for the group to repeat.
3. Repeat words as necessary.

Concept Development Activity

1. Place the **police officer, arrest,** and **court** cards at the front of the room as column headings.
2. Point to each card and have the learners identify the terms.

MATERIALS

Large vocabulary cards (from Lessons A & B)

OK/Not OK cards

Yes/No cards

Picture representing **obey** from Lesson A

3. Group the cards to express the concepts for the lesson according to the groupings below. In group 2, include the picture representing **obey.**

Group 1	Group 2	Group 3
Police	Arrest	Court
Stop	Obey police officer	On time
Ask questions	Ask for free lawyer	Lawyer helps
Arrest	Talk with lawyer	
	Talk with police	

4. Introduce each concept slowly, following the format below, so that the group is able to understand and verbalize each without difficulty.

> **I:** "Stop, ask questions, arrest." (Hold up the **stop, ask, questions,** and **arrest** cards and ask the group to repeat each term.
>
> **G:** "Stop, ask questions, arrest."

5. Place the cards under the **police officer** card heading.
6. Repeat the process with the other concepts, placing the cards for each under the corresponding heading.
7. Repeat each concept more than one time for verbal practice and understanding.

Comprehension Check

1. Shuffle all of the large vocabulary cards and the **obey** picture together.
2. Put all of the large vocabulary cards and the **obey** picture faceup on a table or other visible surface.
3. Call out a term. Ask learners to locate the corresponding card or picture and pick it up from the surface where it is displayed.
4. Repeat the check as necessary to ensure that all learners have a solid understanding of the vocabulary.

Oral Language Activity 4

Introduce the Dialogue

1. Write the sample dialogue (see example on next page) on the board or on chart paper.
2. Read through the dialogue by pointing to each line as it is presented and holding up the corresponding cards and pictures.

Speaker 1:	"What should you do?" (Point to the **obey** picture and **police officer** card. Motion for a response.)
Speaker 2:	"Obey the police officer."
Speaker 1:	"What should you do?" (Point to the **ask, free,** and **lawyer** cards and motion for a response.)
Speaker 2:	"Ask for a free lawyer."
Speaker 1:	"What should you do?" (Point to the **talk** and **lawyer** cards and motion for a response.)
Speaker 2:	"Talk with lawyer."
Speaker 1:	"What should you do?" (Point to the **talk** and **police officer** cards and motion for a response.)
Speaker 2:	"Talk with police officer."

3. Perform the dialogue, with the instructor taking the role of Speaker 1 and the learners responding as Speaker 2.
4. Repeat the dialogue as a group three times.

Dialogue Activity

1. Write the sample dialogue (see example below) on the board or on chart paper and read it for the group, pointing to each word.
2. Introduce the dialogue, asking the target question and having learners respond to visual prompts.

Speaker 1:	"What should you do?" (Point to the **obey** picture and **police officer** card. Motion for a response.)
Speaker 2:	"Obey the police officer."
Speaker 1:	"What should you do?" (Point to the **ask, free,** and **lawyer** cards and motion for a response.)
Speaker 2:	"Ask for a free lawyer."
Speaker 1:	"What should you do?" (Point to the **talk** and **lawyer** cards and motion for a response.)
Speaker 2:	"Talk with lawyer."
Speaker 1:	"What should you do?" (Point to the **talk** and **police officer** cards and motion for a response.)
Speaker 2:	"Talk with police officer."

3. Point to each word whenever the dialogue is repeated in this activity.
4. Perform the dialogue as a group three times.
5. Use the vocabulary cards, mime, or realia to illustrate the dialogue and prompt learners.
6. Assist learners as necessary.

Comprehension Check

1. Hold up two cards (including the **obey** picture) or sets of cards and identify one of the target terms or phrases correctly.
2. Ask the group to point to the correct card(s).

> **I:** "Obey the police officer." (Hold up the **obey** picture and **police officer** card. Hold up the **ask, free,** and **lawyer** cards. Motion for a response.)
>
> **G:** "Obey the police officer." (Learners should point to the **obey** picture and **police officer** card.)

Reading Activity

MATERIALS

Large vocabulary cards

Find the Word activity sheet (one enlarged and one per learner)

Review

1. Shuffle all of the target vocabulary cards.
2. Show each card to the group while pronouncing each word slowly and clearly.
3. Run a finger under each word to help learners begin to recognize the words apart from the pictures.
4. Have the learners repeat the words at least three times.

> **I:** "Arrest." (Point to the word.)
>
> **G:** "Arrest."
>
> **I:** "Arrest." (Underline the word with a finger. Motion for the group to repeat the word.)
>
> **G:** "Arrest."

NOTE

Separating words from pictures should be done gradually and after plenty of practice.

5. Continue to review with the cards, using the pattern above.
6. Fold cards in half to show only the words, to help learners become less dependent on the pictures.
7. Move from group to individual practice as learners become more comfortable reading the words without the assistance of the pictures.

Find the Word Activity

1. Pass out a Find the Word activity sheet to each learner.
2. Post the enlarged copy of the activity sheet in the front of the room.
3. Place a set of vocabulary cards in a visible location, to assist learners.
4. Use item 1 as an example on the enlarged activity sheet to show learners how to complete the activity sheet.
5. Point to the picture in item 1 and have learners identify it verbally.

6. Demonstrate looking at the word choices to show learners how to find the word that corresponds to the picture.
7. Model for learners how to circle the correct word. Have learners circle the correct word on their own activity sheets.

> **I:** "Court." (Motion for learners to look at the word choices and the displayed vocabulary cards. Mime looking for the word *court*.)
>
> **I:** "Here it is. Court." (Circle the corresponding word.)

8. Complete the activity sheet as a group.

Writing Activity

Review

1. Shuffle all of the target vocabulary cards together.
2. Show each card to the group while pronouncing each word slowly and clearly.
3. Run a finger under each word to help learners begin to recognize the words apart from the pictures.
4. Have the learners repeat the words at least three times.

> **I:** "Lawyer." (Point to the word.)
>
> **G:** "Lawyer."
>
> **I:** "Lawyer." (Underline the word with a finger. Motion for the group to repeat the word.)
>
> **G:** "Lawyer."

5. Continue to review with the cards, using the pattern above.
6. Fold cards in half to show only the words, to help learners become less dependent on the pictures.
7. Move from group to individual practice as learners become more comfortable reading the words without the assistance of the pictures.

Fill in the Missing Words Activity

1. Distribute a Fill in the Missing Words activity sheet to each learner.
2. Post an enlarged activity sheet at the front of the room.
3. Place the large vocabulary cards and the **obey** picture in a visible location, to assist learners.
4. Using the enlarged activity sheet, ask the group to look at each concept and identify the pictures.
5. Model for the learners how to write the missing words on the lines, using the displayed large vocabulary cards as a reference.

MATERIALS

Large vocabulary cards

Picture representing **obey** from Lesson A

Fill in the Missing Words activity sheet (one enlarged and one per learner)

NOTE

Separating words from pictures should be done gradually and after plenty of practice.

6. Have learners complete the activity sheet (see groupings below).
7. Assist the group as necessary.

Group 1	Group 2	Group 3
Police	Arrest	Court
Stop	Obey police officer	On time
Ask questions	Ask for free lawyer	Lawyer helps
Arrest	Talk with lawyer	
Stop talking	Talk with police officer	

Unit Review Activity

© New Readers Press. All rights reserved.

MATERIALS

Unit Review activity sheet (one enlarged and one per learner)

Large vocabulary cards (from Lessons A & B)

NOTE

The Unit Review Activity can be done as a group activity for reinforcing the concepts learned in the lesson or done as an individual activity for assessment purposes.

OK or Not OK Review Activity

1. Use large vocabulary cards from Lessons A and B to review the vocabulary and concepts of the unit.
2. Post an enlarged copy of the activity sheet in the front of the room or in another visible location.
3. Point to each picture on the enlarged activity sheet and ask learners to identify it. Make sure learners understand the symbol for No (circle with slash) to indicate that what is pictured is not used.
4. Distribute a copy of the Unit Review activity sheet to each learner.
5. On the enlarged activity sheet, point to the picture or pair of pictures in each item. Elicit from learners whether the action or combination in the item is OK (desirable, legal, or an appropriate action) or Not OK (not desirable, illegal, or an unwise action).
6. Ask learners to complete the activity on their own sheets. If necessary, use the enlarged activity sheet to model for learners how to check the correct column to indicate that the item is OK or Not OK.

Central Theme Picture

Family

✂

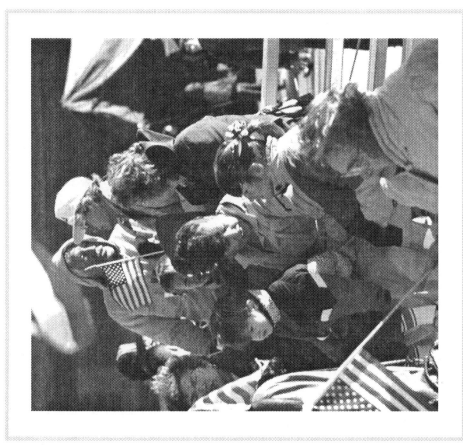

Citizens

Law

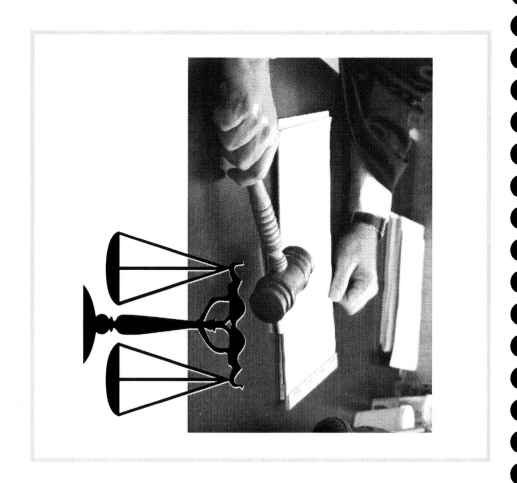

Police officer

Rule

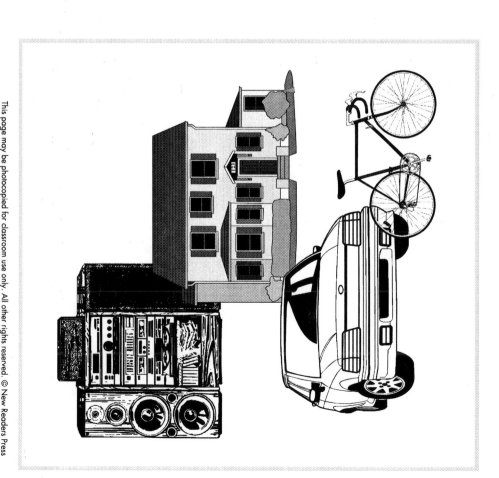

Property

School

People

Picture Bingo Board 1

Picture Bingo Board 2

Picture Bingo Board 3

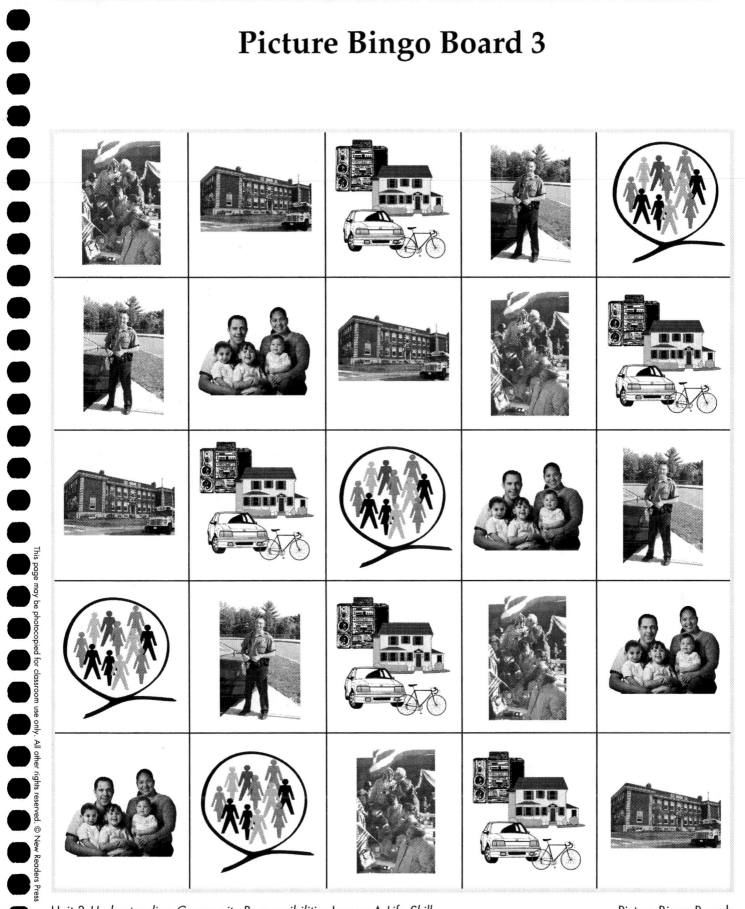

Picture Bingo Board 4

Sentence/Picture Matching Activity

Look at each sentence. Draw a line to the matching group of pictures.

1. Citizens respect property.

2. Citizens obey rules and laws.

3. Citizens help people.

Unit 3 *Understanding Community Responsibilities* Lesson A *Life Skill*

Reading Activity Sheet

Complete the Sentences Activity

Look at the pictures. Write the missing words.

1.

   _____ **respect**

   _____ .

2.

   _____ **obey**

   _____ **and**

   _____ .

3.

   _____ **help**

   _____ .

Lawyer

Court

Large Vocabulary Cards

Unit 3 *Understanding Community Responsibilities:* B

Questions

Free

Ask

Arrest

Stop

Talk

Yes

No

On time

Unit 3 *Understanding Community Responsibilities:* B   Large Vocabulary Cards

Find the Word Activity

Look at each picture. Circle the correct word.

1.	Ask	Court	Free
2.	On time	Stop	Lawyer
3.	Questions	Arrest	Talk
4.	Free	Lawyer	Arrest
5.	Court	On time	Stop
6.	Court	Questions	Free

Fill in the Missing Words Activity

Look at the pictures. Write the missing words.

1. Police

_____ .

_____ questions.

_____ .

_____ talking.

2. Arrest

Obey _____

_____ .

Ask for a _____
lawyer.

Talk with _____ .

Talk with _____ .

3. Court

____ _____ .

_____ helps.

Unit 3 *Understanding Community Responsibilities* Lesson B *Civic Responsibility*   Writing Activity Sheet

Unit Review Activity

Look at each picture or group of pictures. Check OK or Not OK.

	OK	Not OK
1.	_____	_____
2.	_____	_____
3.	_____	_____
4.	_____	_____
5.	_____	_____

Unit 4

Understanding a Lease

Lesson A - Life Skill

How to Rent

VOCABULARY

NOUNS
Lease

Month

Rent

Security deposit

Utilities

Year

VERBS
Pay

Sign

QUESTION
What do you need to do?

Objectives
- To help learners become familiar with the renting process
- To help learners understand what general costs and terms are important when signing a lease

Materials Included
- Large reproducible vocabulary cards
- Sorting activity sheet
- Match the Phrases and Pictures activity sheet
- Complete the Dialogue activity sheet
- **OK/Not OK** cards (page 250)
- **Yes/No** cards

Materials Needed
- An additional instructor copy (enlarged) of the activity sheets
- A long piece of card stock or other instructor-devised method to use as a tapper (one per learner)
- A real or instructor-made replica of a lease
- Large card with the number **1**
- A calendar
- Real or play money
- Real or instructor-made replicas of a money order and utility bills (electric, gas, telephone, and water)
- A checkbook or a real or instructor-made replica of a check
- Pictures representing the various utilities (e.g., picture of a telephone, thermostat, faucet with running water, lamps or electrical appliances, etc.)

Central Theme Picture

Possible Responses
Ad
Document
Man
Newspaper
Paper
Rent
Sign

Introduce the Theme Picture

1. Show learners the theme picture and ask for a response.
2. Encourage learners to say anything about the picture that they can.

> **I:** "What's happening in this picture?" (Point out key things about the picture to elicit a response.)

Oral Language Activity 1

MATERIALS

Large noun cards (two sets, more if necessary to provide each learner with at least one card)

Realia (a lease, a calendar, a money order, a check or checkbook, and utility bills)

Pictures representing the various utilities

Tappers (one per learner and one for the instructor)

Introduce the Target Nouns and Phrases

1. Show each large vocabulary card to the group. Pronounce each word slowly and clearly.

> **I:** "Lease." (Hold up the **lease** card and motion for the learners to repeat.)
> **G:** "Lease."
> **I:** "Lease." (Motion for the group to repeat.)
> **G:** "Lease."
> **I:** "Lease." (Motion for the group to repeat. Put the **lease** card at the front of the room.)
> **G:** "Lease."

2. Introduce the other target nouns using the format above (**month, rent, security deposit, utilities,** and **year**).
3. Use mime, pictures, and realia (see suggestions on next page) as necessary to help the group understand the target nouns.

Suggested Realia

Lease - a copy of a real lease or instructor-made replica

Month - a calendar page showing a full month or a 12-month calendar with a single month circled

Rent - real or instructor-made replica of a money order or a checkbook to show rent paid each month on a specific date

Security deposit - real or instructor-made replica of a money order and receipt of payment

Utilities - copies or instructor-made replicas of electric, gas, water, and telephone bills; pictures representing the various utilities

Year - a 12-month calendar or calendar page with the year circled

4. Say each word and have the group repeat each one three times.
5. Repeat any words more than three times as necessary.

Tap Activity

1. Place each noun card faceup on the table or other available surface so that the cards do not crowd each other or overlap.
2. Pass out tappers (one for each learner).
3. Motion for the learners to listen carefully by holding one hand up with palm open to an ear.
4. Call out a target noun. Ask learners to look for the corresponding card on the table and identify it with a tapper.
5. Motion for the learners to hold up their tappers to begin.

> **I:** "Ready?" (Hold the tapper up.)
> **G:** "OK."
> **I:** "Rent." (Hold up the **rent** card and identify it verbally. Motion for the learners to try to quickly identify the corresponding card and tap it.)

6. Ask the learner whose tapper identifies the correct card first to pick the card up and repeat the noun it represents. The learner keeps the card.

> **L:** "Rent." (Learner holds up the **rent** card.)

7. When all of the cards have been removed from the surface, have each learner identify which cards he or she holds.
8. Repeat any of the nouns learners have trouble remembering.

Comprehension Check

1. Shuffle all of the cards.
2. Distribute the cards to the learners at random. Make sure each learner has at least one card.
3. Call out each target noun and motion for the learner(s) with the corresponding card to hold it up.

NOTE

This activity can be done as a competition. The learner who collects the most cards wins. If the learners cannot remember a noun, say it out loud and have the group repeat it.

4. Continue calling out target vocabulary and motioning for learners to hold up the corresponding cards.
5. Assist the learners as necessary.

Oral Language Activity 2

MATERIALS

Large noun cards (one set for each learner or pair of learners)

Large verb cards (one set for each learner or pair of learners)

Realia (a lease, a calendar, a money order, a check or checkbook, real or play money, and utility bills)

Large card with number **1**

Yes/No cards

Introduce the Target Verbs

1. Show each large verb card to the group while pronouncing each word slowly and clearly.

> **I:** "Pay." (Hold up the **pay** card. Mime the verb **pay** by demonstrating exchanging money for goods, using a book, pens or pencils, or other objects in the room. Motion for the group to repeat the word.)
>
> **G:** "Pay."
>
> **I:** "Good. Pay." (Motion for the group to repeat.)
>
> **G:** "Pay." (Hold up the **pay** card.)
>
> **I:** "Pay." (Motion for the group to repeat. Put the **pay** card at the front of the room.)
>
> **G:** "Pay."

2. Introduce the verb **sign** using the format above.
3. Explain the verb **sign** by demonstrating how to sign various documents (a check, a lease, or a money order) or model signing on the board or on chart paper.
4. Say each word and have the group repeat each one three times.
5. Repeat any terms more than three times as necessary.

Noun and Verb Activity

1. Introduce verb + noun combinations in the order suggested below.
2. Using the vocabulary cards, model how the nouns and verbs should be paired together for this activity.
3. Help learners understand the terms using mime and realia.

Order of Terms and Suggested Realia

1. Sign lease - copy of a lease
2. One year - calendar, **1** card
3. Pay security deposit - money order or check with amount circled
4. Pay rent (month) - money order or check and a calendar
5. Pay utilities - money order or check, and bills for electric, gas, water, or telephone

> **I:** "Sign lease." (Hold up the **sign** and **lease** cards. Hold up a lease. Demonstrate signing the lease. Motion for the group to repeat the term.)
>
> **G:** "Sign lease."
>
> **I:** "Sign lease." (Hold up the **sign** and **lease** cards and the lease. Motion for the group to repeat.)
>
> **G:** "Sign lease."
>
> **I:** "Sign lease." (Hold up the **sign** and **lease** cards and the lease. Motion for the group to repeat.)
>
> **G:** "Sign lease."

4. Have learners repeat each phrase at least three times.
5. Help learners make clear distinctions between phrases.
6. Distribute sets of noun and verb cards to each learner or pair of learners.
7. Have learners combine cards as presented above and place the combinations of cards in the order established by this lesson.
8. Ask the group to identify the phrases represented by the combinations of cards verbally as a group, in pairs, or individually.
9. Have learners use mime and realia or the cards to demonstrate the meaning of each combination of cards.
10. Assist learners as necessary.

Comprehension Check

1. Collect the target noun and verb cards and reshuffle them.
2. Introduce the cards, holding up combinations of nouns and verbs, identifying the combinations correctly and incorrectly at random.
3. Model how to say Yes when the card combination is correctly identified, and No when it is incorrectly identified.

> **I:** "Pay utilities." (Hold up the **pay** and **utilities** cards.)
>
> **I:** "Pay utilities. Yes." (Point to the **pay** and **utilities** cards and nod in agreement. Motion for the learners to repeat.)
>
> **G:** "Yes."
>
> **I:** "One year." (Hold up the **pay** and **utilities** cards again.)
>
> **I:** "One year. No." (Point to the **pay** and **utilities** cards and shake head in motion disagreement. Motion for the learners to repeat.)
>
> **G:** "No."

4. Continue with other noun and verb combinations at random.
5. Repeat terms as necessary.

Oral Language Activity 3

MATERIALS

Large noun cards

Large verb cards

Realia (a lease, a calendar, a money order, a check or checkbook, real or play money, and utility bills)

Large card with number **1**

Sorting activity sheet (one enlarged and one per learner)

Yes/No cards

OK/Not OK cards

Introduce the Dialogue

1. Place the large noun and verb cards at the front of the room or in another visible location.
2. Hold up each card separately and ask the group to identify each term.

> **I:** "What's this?" (Point to the **lease** card and hold up a lease. Motion for a response.)
>
> **G:** "Lease."
>
> **I:** "What's this?" (Point to the **month** card and hold up a calendar page. Motion for the group to respond.)
>
> **G:** "Month."
>
> **I:** "What's this?" (Point to the **rent** card and hold up a money order or check, or point to the amount for rent written on the lease. Motion for the group to respond.)
>
> **G:** "Rent."

3. Have the group respond with the other terms using the format above. Use the vocabulary cards, individually or in combination, with realia, as suggested below.

Other Vocabulary Terms and Suggested Realia

Security deposit - a money order with the amount circled to match the amount on a lease

Utilities - bills for electricity, gas, water, and telephone; pictures representing the various utilities

Year - a calendar

One year - **1** card and a 12-month calendar

Pay security deposit - a money order prepared for paying a security deposit

Pay rent (month) - a money order and a calendar to demonstrate paying rent each month

Pay utilities - a check or money order and bills for various utilities

4. For a complete review of the terms, assist learners as necessary to put nouns and verbs together in the combinations established in this lesson (see Oral Language Activity 2).

Sorting Activity

1. Distribute a Sorting activity sheet to each learner.
2. Place an enlarged Sorting activity sheet at the front of the room or in another visible location. On the enlarged activity sheet, use item 1 as an example to model the activity.

3. Show the group that the purpose of the activity is to decide which combinations of pictures are appropriately marked with Yes or No (OK) and which are inappropriately marked with Yes or No (Not OK).

> **I:** "What's this?" (Point to the **sign lease** pictures on the activity sheet and motion for a response.)
>
> **G:** "Sign lease."
>
> **I:** "Good. Sign lease. Yes." (Point to the **sign lease** pictures and the word Yes.)
>
> **I:** "OK or Not OK?" (Point to the picture and gesture for a response.)
>
> **G:** "OK."
>
> **I:** "Great. Check OK." (Show learners where to place the check mark. Show them they should place it next to the **sign lease** pictures and Yes, under the heading OK.)

4. Continue eliciting the information on the activity sheet from the group and asking if the combinations presented are OK or Not OK (see combinations below).
5. Assist learners as necessary.

Combinations for Activity Sheet

Sign lease/Yes = OK
Sign lease/No = Not OK
Pay utilities/No = Not OK
Pay security deposit/Yes = OK
Pay rent (month)/Yes = OK
Pay rent (month)/No = Not OK

Comprehension Check

1. Distribute a set of **OK/Not OK** cards to each learner.
2. Hold up various sets of cards, paired with Yes or No.
3. Ask learners to identify the combinations as OK or Not OK by holding up the appropriate card.

> **I:** "Pay rent. No." (Motion to the pictures and the **No** card. Gesture for the group to decide if the combination is OK or Not OK. Motion for a response.)
>
> **G:** "Not OK." (Learners should hold up the **Not OK** card.)

4. Motion for the group to say OK or Not OK each time to help reinforce their comprehension.

Oral Language Activity 4

MATERIALS

Large vocabulary cards (one set of cards per learner)

NOTE

Pointing to the couplets while reading is important to do even if the learners are non-readers or nonliterate.

Introduce the Couplet Activity

1. Write the couplets (see example below) on the board or on chart paper.
2. Introduce the couplets by pointing to each line. Take the role of Speaker 1 and ask the target question. Motion for learners to respond as Speaker 2.
3. Prompt learners' response by holding up cards corresponding to the answer in each couplet.

> **Speaker 1:** "What do you need to do?" (Hold up the **sign** and **lease** cards and motion for a response.)
>
> **Speaker 2:** "Sign lease."
>
> **Speaker 1:** "What do you need to do?" (Hold up the **pay** and **security deposit** cards and motion for a response.)
>
> **Speaker 2:** "Pay security deposit."
>
> **Speaker 1:** "What do you need to do?" (Hold up the **pay** and **rent** cards and motion for a response.)
>
> **Speaker 2:** "Pay rent."
>
> **Speaker 1:** "What do you need to do?" (Hold up the **pay** and **utilities** cards and motion for a response.)
>
> **Speaker 2:** "Pay utilities."

4. Make sure that the learners can respond to each prompt before continuing on to the couplet activity.

Couplet Activity

1. Distribute one set of vocabulary cards to each learner.
2. Model the activity, assisting the learners through the first couplet.

> **I:** "What do you need to do?" (Hold up the **sign** and **lease** cards. Motion for learners to respond and to hold up their corresponding cards.)
>
> **G:** "Sign lease." (Learners should hold up the **sign** and **lease** cards in their individual sets as they respond.)

3. Continue with the activity by prompting the learners to respond verbally and hold up the corresponding cards.

> **I:** "What do you need to do?" (Hold up the **pay** and **security deposit** cards and motion for a response.)
>
> **G:** "Pay security deposit." (Learners should hold up the **pay** and **security deposit** cards.)
>
> **I:** "What do you need to do?" (Hold up the **pay** and **rent** cards and motion for a response.)
>
> **G:** "Pay rent." (Learners should hold up the **pay** and **rent** cards.)
>
> **I:** "What do you need to do?" (Hold up the **pay** and **utilities** cards and motion for a response.)
>
> **G:** "Pay utilities." (Learners should hold up the **pay** and **utilities** cards.)

4. Collect, shuffle, and redistribute the cards to the learners for more verbal practice.
5. Repeat couplets as necessary.
6. Assist learners as needed.

Comprehension Check

1. Distribute one set of cards to each learner.
2. Ask the target question. Prompt the learners to respond by holding up combinations of cards to signal the desired response.
3. Ask learners to hold up the corresponding cards and say the correct response.

> **I:** "What do you need to do?" (Hold up the **pay** and **rent** cards. Motion for a response.)
>
> **G:** "Pay rent." (Learners should hold up the **pay** and **rent** cards.)

4. If necessary, demonstrate how learners should hold up the corresponding cards as they respond.
5. Continue with other sets of cards at random to check learners' understanding.

Reading Activity

MATERIALS

Large vocabulary cards

Match the Phrases and Pictures activity sheet (one enlarged and one per learner)

Review

1. Show each card to the group while pronouncing each word slowly and clearly.
2. Run a finger under each word to help learners begin to recognize the words apart from the pictures.
3. Have the learners repeat the words at least three times.

> **I:** "Lease." (Point to the word.)
>
> **G:** "Lease."
>
> **I:** "Lease." (Underline the word with a finger. Motion for the group to repeat the word.)
>
> **G:** "Lease."

4. Continue to review with the cards, using the pattern above.
5. Fold cards in half to show only the words, to help learners become less dependent on the pictures.
6. Move from group to individual practice as learners become more comfortable reading the words without the assistance of the pictures.

Match the Phrases and Pictures Activity

1. Distribute a Match the Phrases and Pictures activity sheet to each learner.
2. Place an enlarged activity sheet at the front of the room or in another visible location.
3. Ask learners to read each phrase in column one and match it to the corresponding pair of pictures in column two.
4. On the enlarged activity sheet, demonstrate that each phrase should be matched to a pair of pictures by drawing a line from a sample phrase in column one to the corresponding pair of pictures in column two.
5. Have learners complete their own activity sheets.
6. Assist learners as needed.

Writing Activity

MATERIALS

Large vocabulary cards

Complete the Dialogue activity sheet (one enlarged and one per learner)

Review

1. Show each card to the group while pronouncing each word slowly and clearly.
2. Run a finger under each word to help learners begin to recognize the words apart from the pictures.
3. Have the learners repeat the words at least three times.

> **I:** "Rent." (Point to the word.)
>
> **G:** "Rent."
>
> **I:** "Rent." (Underline the word with a finger. Motion for the group to repeat the word.)
>
> **G:** "Rent."

4. Continue to review with the cards, using the pattern on the previous page.
5. Fold cards in half to show only the words, to help learners become less dependent on the pictures.
6. Move from group to individual practice as learners become more comfortable reading the words without the assistance of the pictures.

Complete the Dialogue Activity

1. Distribute a Complete the Dialogue activity sheet to each learner.
2. Place an enlarged activity sheet and the vocabulary cards at the front of the room or in another visible location.
3. Show learners that the cards displayed in the room may be used to assist in completing the dialogue.
4. Show learners how to complete the dialogue by writing the correct phrases under the appropriate pictures.
5. Demonstrate writing a phrase in the appropriate place under the pictures on the enlarged activity sheet.
6. Have learners complete their own activity sheets.
7. Have learners practice the dialogue when the activity is completed, by asking the question and pointing to the response to prompt learners.
8. Assist learners as necessary.

Lesson B - Civic Responsibility

B Renters' Rights

VOCABULARY

NOUNS
Electricity
Heat
Landlord (owner)
Maintenance
Trash
Water

VERB PHRASE
Call landlord

Objective
To help learners understand their basic rights as rent payers

Materials Included
- Large reproducible vocabulary cards
- Small reproducible picture cards
- Mini Picture Bingo boards
- Word Search activity sheet
- Fill in the Missing Words activity sheet
- **Yes/No** cards
- **OK/Not OK** cards (page 250)

Materials Needed
- Additional instructor copy (enlarged) of the activity sheets
- Small objects (buttons, coins, dry beans, etc.) to use as bingo board markers
- Pictures of broken and unbroken items in a home, such as a ceiling, a floor, windows, pipes, or major appliances
- Pictures representing utilities (heat, water, electricity), such as a lit lamp, a running faucet, and a furnace, radiator, or thermostat
- Real trash bags or pictures of trash bags or trash cans
- Picture(s) of man or woman to represent a landlord
- A real or toy telephone
- Real or instructor-made replica of a lease
- A bottle of water or picture of a sink, bathtub, or shower

Civics Introduction

Renters' Rights

Individuals who pay rent for an apartment or house should know their rights with regard to water, heat, and electricity, especially if these utilities are included in their rental agreement. A landlord cannot refuse to repair problems that are hazardous or that threaten the renter's quality of life, because routine maintenance is a component of a landlord's responsibility as a property owner. Renters' rights also include being able to permit access to friends, family, or others without needing permission from a landlord. Renters cannot be evicted without being served legal documentation, and a landlord cannot change locks to prevent entry by the renter without following local legal procedures. Similarly, a landlord cannot remove a renter's items from the property without following necessary legal procedures.

This topic is important to newly arrived non-English-speaking adults, who commonly live in rental properties. Because of language difficulties, these renters can misunderstand their own obligations (as presented in Lesson A) and may not realize the obligations of the landlord. They need to be aware of those obligations and understand when they should (or should not) contact the landlord to get necessary repairs made.

This topic is of special importance to non-English-speaking workers, such as migrant farm workers, who may live in housing provided by farm owners or employers. This housing is often considered to be part of their wages. Even though money for rent is not exchanged between the employee and employer, the rights and obligations of people in this situation are the same as the rights and obligations of parties to a lease or rental agreement.

While Lesson A presents a situation in which utilities are paid by the renter, Lesson B presents rental situations in which basic utilities are included in the rent. It also focuses on the landlord's obligation to provide basic maintenance to the property. It is important for new arrivals to be aware of their legal rights concerning renting space for personal and/or commercial use. Knowledge of their rights as renters is helpful for new arrivals' success in the community, as it helps prevent possible exploitation or mistreatment from landlords.

Oral Language Activity 1

MATERIALS

Large noun cards

Small picture cards

Mini Picture Bingo boards

Bingo board markers

Pictures representing utilities and various maintenance items, such as trash

Introduce the Target Nouns

1. Hold up each target noun card, pronouncing each word slowly and clearly.
2. Motion for learners to repeat each word.
3. Use realia, pictures, and mime as necessary to connect each noun with the learners' prior knowledge.

> **I:** "Heat." (Hold up the **heat** card. Motion for the group to repeat.)
>
> **G:** "Heat."
>
> **I:** "Heat." (Hold up a picture of a furnace, thermostat, or radiator, and motion for the group to repeat.)
>
> **G:** "Heat."
>
> **I:** "Heat." (Hold up the **heat** card and the picture. Motion for the group to repeat.)
>
> **G:** "Heat."

4. Use the vocabulary cards in combination with pictures or realia (see suggestions below) to introduce the other target nouns.

Other Suggested Pictures and Realia

Maintenance - pictures of broken and unbroken items (a ceiling, walls, floors, pipes, or electrical problems) or of home repairs being done

Trash - filled trash bags or pictures of trash bags or trash cans

Water - bottle of water, picture of sink, bathtub, or shower

5. Have learners repeat each word at least three times.
6. Repeat pronunciation and practice the words more than three times as necessary.

Mini Picture Bingo

1. Pass out one bingo board and a set of bingo board markers to each learner.
2. Demonstrate that the purpose of the activity is to mark three boxes in a row (horizontally, vertically, or diagonally).
3. Mix up the small picture cards and place them in a container (a basket, box, or envelope) so that learners can choose them easily.
4. Choose a card from the container at random and show it to the group. Identify the picture verbally.
5. Motion for learners to repeat words as pictures are drawn from the container.
6. Continue to model, drawing one or more noun cards to help the learners understand the activity.

NOTE

More than one copy of each card may be used so that each learner can draw a card at least once.

7. Have the learners take turns drawing cards from the container and identifying each vocabulary term.
8. Assist learners in finding the correct pictures on their bingo boards.
9. Have learners put instructor-provided markers on the correct pictures on their boards.
10. Walk around the room to check each learner's card.
11. Ask learners to call out *Bingo* once they have marked three boxes in a row (horizontally, vertically, or diagonally).
12. Have learners review nouns verbally once the activity is complete.

Comprehension Check

1. Hold up two noun cards and identify one correctly.
2. Ask learners to point to the correct card.
3. Motion for the group to repeat the word.

> **I:** "Water." (Hold up the **water** and **heat** card. Motion for a response.)
>
> **G:** "Water." (Learners should point to the **water** card.)

4. Continue to check with other pairs of noun cards.

Oral Language Activity 2

Introduce Rental Situations

1. Hold up combinations of cards and associate the scenarios they represent with OK or Not OK.

> **I:** "What's this?" (Hold up the **heat** card. Hold up the **Yes** card.)
>
> **G:** "Heat."
>
> **I:** "Heat. Yes." (Hold up the **heat** and **Yes** cards. Hold up the **OK** card. Motion for the group to repeat OK.)
>
> **G:** "OK."
>
> **I:** "Good. What's this?" (Point to the **water** card. Motion for a response.)
>
> **G:** "Water."
>
> **I:** "Water. No." (Hold up the **water** and **No** cards. Hold up the **Not OK** card. Motion for the group to repeat Not OK.)
>
> **G:** "Not OK."

MATERIALS

Large noun cards (two sets)

OK/Not OK cards

Yes/No cards (3 copies of each card)

2. Continue presenting various scenarios that pair the noun cards
with Yes or No and indicate if each scenario is OK or Not OK.

Scenarios

Heat/Yes = OK
Heat/No = Not OK
Water/Yes = OK
Water/No = Not OK
Maintenance/Yes = OK
Maintenance/No = Not OK
Electricity/Yes = OK
Electricity/No = Not OK

OK or Not OK Concentration

1. Shuffle the two sets of the **heat, electricity, water,** and
maintenance cards and place these cards facedown on the table
or other available surface so that they are not overlapping or
crowding each other.
2. Shuffle the **Yes** and **No** cards separately and place them facedown
on the table or other available surface in the same manner but
keep them separate from the noun cards.
3. Show the group that each learner will choose one card from each
group of cards to turn over.
4. Have the group identify the cards verbally and decide if the
scenario is OK or Not OK.
5. Use the scenarios presented above as the basis for learner
response.

> **I:** "What's this?" (Turn over the **heat** card. Motion for a
> response.)
> **G:** "Heat."
> **I:** "What's this?" (Turn over a **Yes** card. Motion for a
> response.)
> **G:** "Yes."
> **I:** "Heat. Yes. OK or Not OK?" (Motion for a response.)
> **G:** "OK."

6. Have learners follow the format above for turning over cards,
identifying them, and responding with OK or Not OK.
7. Assist learners as necessary.

Comprehension Check

1. Hold up cards representing the scenarios and label them
correctly or incorrectly with the **OK** or **Not OK** cards.
2. Ask the learners to decide if the scenarios are labeled correctly or
incorrectly.

> **I:** "Heat. Yes. OK" (Motion for a response.)
>
> **G:** "Yes."
>
> **I:** "Heat. Yes. Not OK." (Motion for a response.)
>
> **G:** "No. Heat. Yes. OK."

Oral Language Activity 3

MATERIALS

Large verb phrase card

Large noun cards

Pictures of man or woman to represent a landlord

Real or toy telephone

Real or instructor-made replica of a lease

Yes/No cards

Introduce the Verb Phrase

1. Hold up the verb phrase card and pronounce each word slowly and clearly. Motion for learners to repeat the phrase.
2. Use realia, pictures, and mime to explain the meaning of the words.
3. If necessary to clarify meaning, say each word separately, pointing to the appropriate part of the picture on the verb phrase card and using mime and realia to convey meaning.

> **I:** "Call landlord." (Hold up the **call landlord** card. Motion for the group to repeat.)
>
> **G:** "Call landlord."
>
> **I:** "Call landlord." (Hold up the **call landlord** card and motion for the group to repeat.)
>
> **G:** "Call landlord."
>
> **I:** "Call landlord." (Hold up the **call landlord** card. Motion for the group to repeat.)
>
> **G:** "Call landlord."

4. Have learners repeat the phrase at least three times.

Suggested Realia and Mime Ideas

Call landlord - use a telephone and a lease paired with a picture of a man or woman to demonstrate **call landlord.**

5. Repeat pronunciation and practice the term more than three times as necessary.

Call Landlord Activity

1. Place the **call landlord** card on the board or other visible surface.
2. Make OK and Not OK columns next to the **call landlord** card.
3. Associate OK or Not OK as appropriate with rental situations to make sure that the group understands when the landlord should be called.
4. Pair nouns (**water, heat, electricity,** or **maintenance**) with Yes or No, as in Oral Language Activity 2.

5. Associate the **call landlord** card when the pair suggests that the water, electricity, or heater is not working or that maintenance is not being done.

> **I:** "Water. Yes. OK." (Hold up the **water, YES,** and **OK** cards. Motion for the group to repeat.)
>
> **G:** "Water. Yes. OK."
>
> **I:** "No water. Not OK. Call landlord." (Hold up the **No, water,** and **Not OK** cards. Add the **call landlord** card. Motion for the group to repeat.)
>
> **G:** "No water. Not OK. Call landlord."

6. Continue with various pairings to help reinforce the principle that basic services that need repair require making a call to the landlord.

Comprehension Check

1. Hold up sets of cards to check the group's understanding of the concept that when utilities (heat, electricity, or water) are not working, the landlord should be called.

> **I:** "No water. Call landlord." (Hold up the **No, water,** and **call landlord** cards.)
>
> **I:** "No water. Call landlord. OK or Not OK?" (Motion for a response.)
>
> **G:** "OK."

2. Check learners' understanding using the **heat** card and by grouping the **water, heat,** and **Yes** cards to make sure that the group understands that they should not call the landlord when utilities are working.
3. Continue to check learners' understanding of **electricity** using the same format.

Oral Language Activity 4

Introduce the Couplets

1. Write the couplets (see next page) on the board or on chart paper.
2. Introduce the couplets to the group, pronouncing each word slowly and clearly and pointing to each word while reading.

MATERIALS

Large vocabulary cards (one set for instructor and enough to give each learner or pair of learners at least one card)

No cards (one for instructor and one for each learner or pair of learners)

Speaker 1: "What's wrong?" (Hold up the **No** and **water** cards. Motion for a response.)

Speaker 2: "No water." (Point to the **No** and **water** cards.)

Speaker 1: "What's wrong?" (Hold up the **No** and **heat** cards. Motion for the group to respond.)

Speaker 2: "No heat." (Point to the **No** and **heat** cards.)

Speaker 1: "What's wrong?" (Hold up the **No** and **electricity** cards. Motion for the group to respond.)

Speaker 2: "No electricity." (Point to the **No** and **electricity** cards.)

Speaker 1: "What's wrong?" (Hold up the **No** and **maintenance** cards. Motion for the group to respond.)

Speaker 2: "No maintenance." (Point to the **No** and **maintenance** cards.)

Speaker 1: "What should you do?" (Hold up the **call landlord** card. Motion for a response.)

Speaker 2: "Call landlord." (Point to the **call landlord** card.)

3. Repeat each question and answer combination at least three times.

Couplet Activity

1. Ask each target question. Use the vocabulary cards when presenting each question to prompt the correct responses.
2. Point to individual words in the couplets as they are modeled for the group.
3. Ask each question and motion for the group to respond to the verbal and visual prompts.

> **I:** "What's wrong?" (Hold up the **No** and **heat** cards. Motion for the group to respond.)
>
> **G:** "No heat." (Point to the **No** and **heat** cards.)

4. Have learners practice the couplets as a group at least three times.
5. Distribute sets of cards to each learner or to pairs of learners. Give at least one noun card or verb phrase card and a No card to each learner or pair with a noun card.
6. Have pairs or individuals respond to the visual and verbal prompts.

> **I:** "What's wrong?" (Hold up the **No** and **water** cards. Motion to the learners holding the corresponding cards to respond.)
>
> **G:** "No water." (Hold up the **No** and **water** cards.)

7. Continue with all noun cards and the verb phrase card, using the format on the previous page.
8. Assist learners as necessary.

Comprehension Check

1. Hold up two sets of cards and identify one correctly.
2. Ask the group to point to the correct set of cards and repeat the term as a group.

> **I:** "No water." (Hold up the **No** and **water** cards and the **No** and **maintenance** cards.)
>
> **G:** "No water." (Learners should point to the **No** and **water** cards.)

Reading Activity

© New Readers Press. All rights reserved.

MATERIALS

Large vocabulary cards

Word Search activity sheet (one enlarged and one per learner)

Review

1. Show each card to the group while pronouncing each word slowly and clearly.
2. Run a finger under each word to help learners begin to recognize the words apart from the pictures.
3. Have the learners repeat the words at least three times.

> **I:** "Maintenance." (Point to the word.)
>
> **G:** "Maintenance."
>
> **I:** "Maintenance." (Underline the word with a finger. Motion for the group to repeat the word.)
>
> **G:** "Maintenance."

NOTE

Separating words from pictures should be done gradually and after plenty of practice.

4. Continue to review with the cards, using the pattern above.
5. Fold cards in half to show only the words, to help learners become less dependent on the pictures.
6. Move from group to individual practice as learners become more comfortable reading the words without the assistance of the pictures.

Word Search Activity

1. Pass out a Word Search activity sheet to each learner.
2. Place an enlarged copy of the activity sheet at the front of the room or in another visible location.
3. On the enlarged activity sheet, show learners how to use the pictures and words listed to locate words in the word search puzzle.
4. Choose a word or phrase from the list to locate in the word search.

5. Read the word or prase for the learners and point to the picture that represents it.
6. Demonstrate how to look in the word search for the word or phrase written under the pictures. On the enlarged activity sheet, model how to circle the item within the word search.
7. Have the learners say each item from the list before they begin their search. Have them circle the item on their own activity sheets.
8. Assist learners as necessary.

Writing Activity

MATERIALS

Large vocabulary cards

OK/Not OK cards

Fill in the Missing Words activity sheet (one enlarged and one per learner)

Review

1. Show each card to the group while pronouncing each word slowly and clearly.
2. Run a finger under each word to help learners begin to recognize the words apart from the pictures.
3. Have the learners repeat the words at least three times.

> **I:** "Water." (Point to the word.)
> **G:** "Water."
> **I:** "Water." (Underline the word with a finger. Motion for the group to repeat the word.)
> **G:** "Water."

NOTE

Separating words from pictures should be done gradually and after plenty of practice.

4. Continue to review with the cards, using the pattern above.
5. Fold cards in half to show only the words, to help learners become less dependent on the pictures.
6. Move from group to individual practice as learners become more comfortable reading the words without the assistance of the pictures.

Fill in the Missing Words Activity

1. Place the large noun and verb cards in the front of the room or in another visible location.
2. Place an enlarged copy of the activity sheet at the front of the room or in another visible location.
3. Pass out a Fill in the Missing Words activity sheet to each learner.
4. Demonstrate how the group can use the posted cards to help them fill in the missing words on the activity sheet by copying the words from the cards and writing on the lines next to the pictures. Show how the example words are written in item 1.
5. Ask the learners to check OK or Not OK based on the situations represented on the activity sheet.

Unit Review Activity

MATERIALS

Unit Review activity sheet (one enlarged and one per learner)

Large vocabulary cards (from Lessons A and B)

NOTE

The Unit Review Activity can be done as a group activity for reinforcing the concepts learned in the lesson or done as an individual activity for assessment purposes.

Unit Review Activities

1. Use the large vocabulary cards from Lessons A and B to review the vocabulary and concepts from the unit.
2. Distribute a copy of the Unit Review activity sheet to each learner. Post an enlarged copy of the activity sheet in the front of the room.
3. On the enlarged activity sheet, point to each pair of pictures in the top activity and have learners identify the action represented by the pictures.
4. Review with learners the correct order of actions presented in Lesson A. Learners can indicate the order by saying numbers, holding up an appropriate number of fingers, or writing a number on a piece of paper and holding it up.
5. Ask learners to complete the activity at the top of the page. If necessary, use the enlarged activity sheet to model numbering the items in the correct order.
6. Review the pictures at the bottom of the page. Have learners identify the phrase or scenario in each one.
7. Point to each of the three scenarios. For each one, ask learners if it is appropriate to call the landlord.
8. Have learners circle the picture representing the scenario for which they should call the landlord. Ask a volunteer to come to the front of the room and circle the answer on the enlarged activity sheet.
9. Assist learners as necessary.

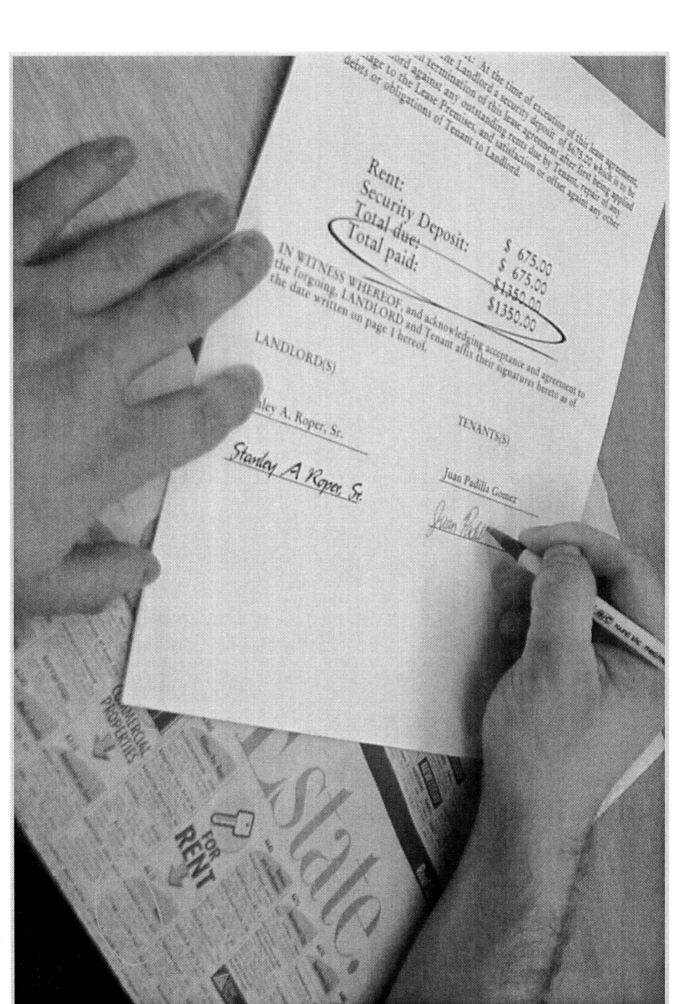

Month

✂

Lease

Rent

Security deposit

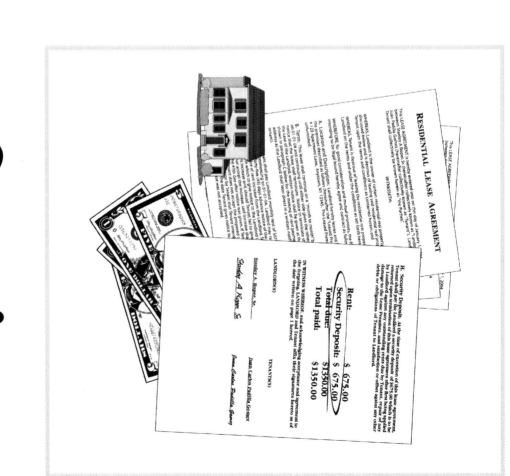

Year

JANUARY FEBRUARY MARCH
APRIL MAY JUNE
JULY AUGUST SEPTEMBER
OCTOBER NOVEMBER DECEMBER

Utilities

Pay

Sign

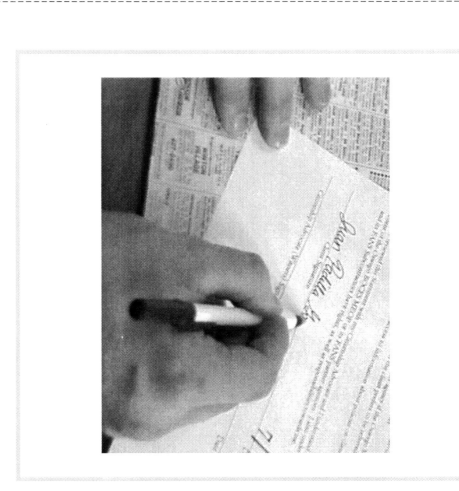

Sorting Activity

Look at the pictures. Check OK or Not OK.

		OK	Not OK
1.	**Yes**	_____	_____
2.	**No**	_____	_____
3.	**No**	_____	_____
4.	**Yes**	_____	_____
5.	**Yes**	_____	_____
6.	**No**	_____	_____

Unit 4 *Understanding a Lease* Lesson A *Life Skill*

Activity Sheet

Match the Phrases and Pictures Activity

Read each phrase. Draw a line to the matching pictures.

1. **Sign lease**

2. **Pay security deposit**

3. **Pay rent**

4. **Pay utilities**

Reading Activity Sheet

Complete the Dialogue Activity

Look at the pictures. Write the missing words. Complete the dialogue.

1. <u>Speaker 1:</u> What do you need to do?

   <u>Speaker 2:</u>

   _____ _____

2. <u>Speaker 1:</u> What do you need to do?

   <u>Speaker 2:</u>

   _____ _____ _____

3. <u>Speaker 1:</u> What do you need to do?

   <u>Speaker 2:</u>

   _____ _____

4. <u>Speaker 1:</u> What do you need to do?

   <u>Speaker 2:</u>

   _____ _____

Heat

✂ -

Maintenance

Landlord
(owner)

Unit 4 *Understanding a Lease* Lesson B

Electricity

Unit 4 *Understanding a Lease* Lesson B

Trash

✂ -

Water

Yes

No

✂

Call landlord

Large Vocabulary Cards

Unit 4 *Understanding a Lease* Lesson B

Unit 4 *Understanding a Lease:* B   Small Picture Cards

Unit 4 *Understanding a Lease:* B   Small Picture Cards

Unit 4 *Understanding a Lease:* B   Small Picture Cards

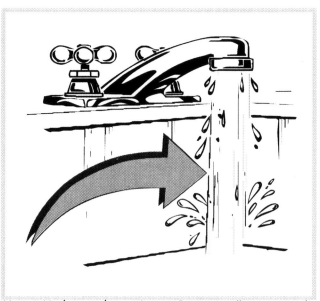

Unit 4 *Understanding a Lease:* B   Small Picture Cards

Unit 4 *Understanding a Lease:* B   Small Picture Cards

Unit 4 *Understanding a Lease:* B   Small Picture Cards

188

Mini Picture Bingo   Board 1

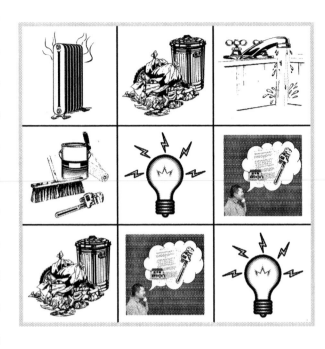

Mini Picture Bingo   Board 2

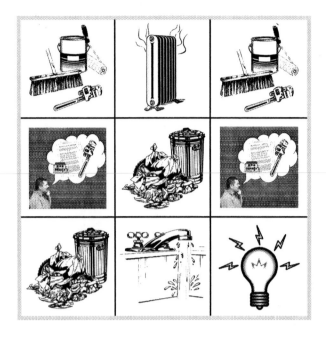

Mini Picture Bingo   Board 3

Mini Picture Bingo   Board 4

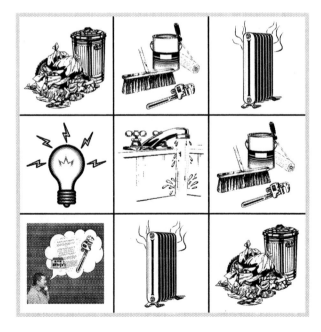

Word Search Activity

Look at the pictures. Find the terms in the puzzle. Circle the words.

Heat

Maintenance

Trash

Water

Call landlord

Electricity

m	a	i	n	t	e	n	a	n	c	e	f	h	n	u
f	y	m	s	h	e	a	t	f	o	u	b	e	i	h
k	d	o	j	k	b	s	n	k	n	z	d	r	k	t
y	c	a	l	l	a	n	d	l	o	r	d	f	j
s	f	g	c	t	x	j	l	s	l	o	p	b	u	u
q	z	o	t	s	t	c	f	u	r	t	r	a	s	h
i	d	m	e	l	e	c	t	r	i	c	i	t	y	b
p	a	l	y	u	o	p	w	a	t	e	r	f	g	x
g	x	d	o	u	m	u	t	h	n	l	i	k	u	s

Reading Activity Sheet

Fill in the Missing Words Activity

Look at the pictures. Write the words. Check OK or Not OK for each situation.

	OK	Not OK
1. No  <u>No maintenance</u>	_____	_____
2. _____	_____	_____
3. No  ___ _____	_____	_____
4. No ___ _____	_____	_____
5.  _____	_____	_____

Number the groups of pictures in the correct order from Lesson A.

_____   _____

_____   _____

Circle the correct picture.

Yes   No   Yes

Unit 5

Maintaining Housing

Lesson A - Life Skill

Home Maintenance

VOCABULARY

NOUNS
Electricity
Gas
Heater
Lock
Refrigerator
Shower
Sink
Stove
Toilet
Water
Window

ADJECTIVES
Not working
Working

Objective
Learners will understand the vocabulary for basic home maintenance problems

Materials Included
- Central theme picture
- Large reproducible vocabulary cards
- Small reproducible picture cards
- Small reproducible word cards
- Picture Bingo boards
- Working/Not Working checklist
- **Yes/No** cards

Materials Needed
- Additional instructor copy (enlarged) of the activity sheets
- Small objects (buttons, coins, dry beans, etc.) to use as bingo board markers
- Pictures of appliances, plumbing fixtures, windows and doors, and items representing utilities (heat, water, electricity)
- Paired household items that are functioning and not functioning, to demonstrate target adjectives (e.g., clock, flashlight, tape player)
- A plunger

Central Theme Picture

MATERIALS

Theme picture

POSSIBLE RESPONSES

Bag

Boy

Clean

Door

House

Outside

Trash

Introduce the Theme Picture

1. Show learners the theme picture and ask for a response.
2. Encourage learners to say anything about the picture that they can.

> **I:** "What's happening in this picture?" (Point out key things about the picture to elicit a response.)

Oral Language Activity 1

MATERIALS

Large noun cards (for items on bingo boards, as indicated in activity)

Pictures of target nouns

Picture Bingo boards

Bingo markers

Yes/No cards

Introduce the Target Nouns

1. Use the cards for the target nouns pictured on the bingo boards (**heater, lock, refrigerator, sink, shower, stove, toilet,** and **window**).
2. Show each large vocabulary card to the group while pronouncing each word slowly and clearly.

> **I:** "Heater." (Hold up the **heater** card and motion for learners to repeat.)
>
> **G:** "Heater."
>
> **I:** "Heater." (Motion for the group to repeat.)
>
> **G:** "Heater."
>
> **I:** "Heater." (Motion for the group to repeat. Put the **heater** card at the front of the room or in another visible location.)
>
> **G:** "Heater."

3. Introduce the target nouns using the format above.
4. Use pictures and mime as necessary to help the group understand the target nouns.
5. Say each word and have the group repeat each one three times.
6. Repeat any words more than three times as necessary.

Picture Bingo Activity

1. Distribute a Picture Bingo board and a set of bingo board markers to each learner.
2. Demonstrate that the purpose of the activity is to mark three boxes in a row (horizontally, vertically, or diagonally).

3. Select the cards for the target nouns pictured on the bingo boards (**heater, lock, refrigerator, sink, shower, stove, toilet,** and **window**) and place them in a pile facedown on the table.
4. Choose a card from the pile at random and show it to the group. Say the word and motion for the learners to repeat.
5. Demonstrate for learners how to find the picture corresponding to the card on their bingo boards and mark it with a bingo marker.
6. Model choosing one or more additional noun cards to help the learners understand the activity.
7. Have the learners take turns drawing cards and identifying each vocabulary term.
8. Assist learners in finding the correct pictures of the nouns on the bingo boards.
9. Have learners put bingo markers on the correct pictures on their boards. Walk around the room to check each learner's card.
10. Ask learners to call out *Bingo* once they have marked three boxes in a row (horizontally, vertically, or diagonally).
11. Have learners review nouns verbally once the activity is complete.

Comprehension Check

1. Hold up each noun card and ask the group to identify each noun.
2. Continue to hold up the same card and ask individuals to respond one by one.

> **I:** "What's this?" (Hold up the **refrigerator** card. Motion for the learners to respond as a group.)
>
> **G:** "Refrigerator."
>
> **I:** "Great. What's this?" (Hold up the **refrigerator** card and motion for each individual learner to respond.)
>
> **L:** "Refrigerator."

3. Repeat with the other vocabulary cards, moving from group to individual practice to ensure comprehension.

Oral Language Activity 2

MATERIALS

Large noun cards (multiple sets, if necessary, to give at least one card to each learner)

Yes/No cards (one set per learner)

Pictures of appliances, plumbing supplies, and other items representing utilities

NOTE

Duplicate cards for **stove** and **heater** will be necessary to complete the sorting activity.

Introduce the Remaining Target Nouns

1. Show each of the remaining large noun cards (**electricity, gas,** and **water**) to the group while pronouncing each word slowly and clearly.

> **I:** "Electricity." (Hold up the **electricity** card. Motion for the learners to repeat the word.)
> **G:** "Electricity."
> **I:** "Electricity." (Motion for the group to repeat.)
> **G:** "Electricity."
> **I:** "Electricity." (Motion for the group to repeat. Put the **electricity** card at the front of the room.)
> **G:** "Electricity."

2. Introduce the other target nouns using the format above.
3. Use mime and pictures as necessary to help the group understand the target nouns.
4. Say each word and have the group repeat each one three times.
5. Repeat any words more than three times as necessary.

Sorting Activity

1. Make three columns on the board or on chart paper.
2. Head each column with one of the target noun cards representing a utility (**electricity, gas,** and **water**).
3. Shuffle selected noun cards (**heater, refrigerator, sink, shower, stove,** and **toilet**).
4. Review the column headings and the remaining words with learners, and have them identify the correct column for each noun card.

> **I:** "Electricity. Gas. Water." (Point to the label on each column. Say the word and motion for the group to repeat.)
> **G:** "Electricity. Gas. Water."
> **I:** "What's this?" (Hold up the **sink** card and motion for the group to respond.)
> **G:** "Sink."
> **I:** "Electricity, gas, or water?" (Point to each column and motion for the group to choose one that corresponds to **sink.**)
> **G:** "Water."
> **I:** "Good. Sink. Water." (Attach the **sink** card to the board or chart paper in the **water** column.)

5. Reshuffle the cards and distribute them among the learners.

6. Ask the learners to hold up their cards one by one and say the word for the item on each card.
7. Have learners decide whether the cards should be placed in the **electricity, gas,** or **water** columns (see suggestions below).
8. Make sure that learners understand that **stove** and **heater** can fall in both the **electricity** and **gas** columns.
9. Have learners place their cards in the correct columns.
10. Assist learners as necessary.

Suggested Columns and Cards

Electricity	Gas	Water
Heater	Heater	Sink
Refrigerator	Stove	Shower
Stove		Toilet

Comprehension Check

1. Give each learner a set of **Yes/No** cards.
2. Place the column headings from Oral Language Activity 2 (**electricity, gas,** and **water**) at the front of the room or in an other visible location.
3. Shuffle the remaining noun cards and hold a card up under the correct column.

> **I:** "Sink. Water. Yes or No?" (Motion for the group to respond with the **Yes** or **No** cards.)
>
> **G:** "Yes." (Learners should hold up the **Yes** card.)

4. Repeat the process with another noun card and hold it up under the incorrect column.

> **I:** "Sink. Electricity. Yes or No?" (Motion for the group to respond with the **Yes** or **No** cards.)
>
> **G:** "No." (Learners should hold up the **No** card.)

5. Repeat the process with all of the noun cards, showing correct and incorrect combinations at random.

Oral Language Activity 3

MATERIALS

Large noun cards (two sets, each copied onto a different color of paper)

Large adjective cards

Paired items that are functioning and not functioning, to demonstrate target adjectives

Yes/No cards (one card per learner)

Introduce the Target Adjectives

1. Show each large adjective card (**working** and **not working**) to the group while pronouncing each word slowly and clearly.

> **I:** "Working." (Hold up the **working** card and motion for the learners to repeat the word.)
>
> **G:** "Working."
>
> **I:** "Working." (Motion for the group to repeat.)
>
> **G:** "Working."
>
> **I:** "Working." (Motion for the group to repeat. Put the **working** card at the front of the room.)
>
> **G:** "Working."

2. Introduce **not working** using the method above.
3. Use functioning and nonfunctioning items to clarify the meaning of the terms.
4. Say each word and have the group repeat each one three times.
5. Make sure that the group can identify **working** and **not working** without assistance.

Working or Not Working Activity

1. Have the learners form a large circle around a table or other available surface.
2. Make two circles of yarn and label one circle *working* and one *not working* using the cards.
3. Use the two colored sets of target noun cards (**heater, lock, refrigerator, sink, shower, stove, toilet,** and **window**). Associate one color with the concept of **working** and the other with **not working,** e.g., blue cards = **working** and orange cards = **not working.**
4. Shuffle both sets of cards together and place the pile facedown on the table in the center of the group.
5. Have each learner take a turn and choose a card from the pile.
6. Use the word from one learner's card to model the activity with the target sentences (see example on the next page).
7. Use the example sentences on the next page and model them for the group, pronouncing each word slowly and clearly. Have the group repeat the sentences at least three times.

> **I:** "Sink. The sink is working." (Point to the **sink** card held up by a learner. Motion to the circle of yarn labeled **working.** Motion for the learner to place the card in the circle.)
>
> **I:** "The sink is working." (Point to the card in the **working** circle. Motion for the group to repeat.)
>
> **G:** "The sink is working."

or

> **I:** "Sink. The sink is not working." (Point to the **sink** card held up by a learner. Motion to the circle of yarn labeled **not working.** Motion for the learner to place the **sink** card in the circle.)
>
> **I:** "The sink is not working." (Point to the **sink** card in the **not working** circle. Motion for the group to repeat.)
>
> **G:** "The sink is not working."

8. Continue by having each learner draw a card. State a complete sentence (**working** or **not working**), using the word on the learner's card. Ask learners to place the cards in the correct circle of yarn (**working** or **not working**) based on the stated sentence.
9. Assist learners as necessary.

Comprehension Check

1. Distribute the **Yes** and **No** cards to the group at random.
2. Use the **working/not working** cards in conjunction with the noun cards to check learners' understanding.
3. Model the activity to help learners associate Yes with a matching combination of sentence plus **working** or **not working** card and No with a combination that does not match (as in the examples below).
4. Have learners respond by saying Yes or No based on the combination provided. Have those learners with the corresponding **Yes** or **No** cards hold them up.

> **I:** "The refrigerator is not working." (Hold up the **refrigerator** and the **not working** cards. Motion for the group to respond.)
>
> **G:** "Yes"
>
> **I:** "The refrigerator is working." (Hold up the **refrigerator** and the **not working** cards. Motion for the group to respond.)
>
> **G:** "No."

5. Alternate correct (matching) and incorrect (not matching) combinations to check learners' comprehension.

Oral Language Activity 4

MATERIALS

Large noun cards

Large adjective cards

NOTE

Pointing to each word while reading is important to do even if the learners are non-readers or nonliterate.

Introduce the Dialogue

1. Write the sample dialogue (see example below) on the board or on chart paper.
2. Read each line for the group, running a finger slowly under each phrase as the words are read.

Speaker 1: "What's wrong?" (Hold up the **stove, refrigerator,** and **heater** cards, the **electricity** card, and the **not working** card. Motion for a response.)

Speaker 2: "The electricity is not working."

Speaker 1: "What's wrong?" (Hold up the **stove** and **heater** cards, the **gas** card, and the **not working** card. Motion for a response.)

Speaker 2: "The gas is not working."

Speaker 1: "What's wrong?" (Hold up the **sink** and **shower** cards, the **water** card, and the **not working** card. Motion for a response.)

Speaker 2: "The water is not working."

Speaker 1: "What's wrong?" (Hold up the **lock** or **window** card and the **not working** card. Motion for a response.)

Speaker 2: "The lock (window) is not working."

3. Perform the dialogue with the instructor taking the role of Speaker 1 and the learners responding as Speaker 2. Prompt or model responses for learners as necessary.
4. Practice the entire dialogue at least three times.

Dialogue Activity

1. Write the sample dialogue (see example below) on the board or on chart paper and read it for the group, pointing to each word.

Speaker 1: "What's wrong?" (Hold up the **stove, refrigerator,** and **heater** cards, the **electricity** card, and the **not working** card. Motion for a response.)

Speaker 2: "The electricity is not working."

Speaker 1: "What's wrong?" (Hold up the **stove** and **heater** cards, the **gas** card, and the **not working** card. Motion for a response.)

Speaker 2: "The gas is not working."

Speaker 1: "What's wrong?" (Hold up the **sink** and **shower** cards, the **water** card, and the **not working** card. Motion for a response.)

Speaker 2: "The water is not working."

Speaker 1: "What's wrong?" (Hold up the **lock** or **window** card and the **not working** card. Motion for a response.)

Speaker 2: "The lock (window) is not working."

2. Point to each word whenever the dialogue is repeated in this activity.
3. Introduce the dialogue, and then perform it with the instructor taking the role of Speaker 1 and the group responding as Speaker 2.
4. Perform the dialogue three times, assisting learners as necessary.

Comprehension Check

1. Place the vocabulary cards faceup on the table or on another available surface where the learners can reach them.
2. Say sentences to the learners, as in the example below. Have them select and hold up the corresponding cards.

> **I:** "The lock is not working." (Motion for the group to find the cards.)
>
> **L:** "The lock is not working." (Learners should hold up the **lock** and **not working** cards.)

3. Continue with other sentences and ask learners to identify the corresponding cards.

Example Sentences

The refrigerator is working.
The sink is not working.
The water is not working.
The gas is working.
The stove is not working.

Reading Activity

MATERIALS

Large vocabulary cards

Small picture cards (multiple sets, if necessary, to give each learner one card)

Review

1. Shuffle all of the large noun cards together.
2. Show each card to the group while pronouncing each word slowly and clearly.
3. Run a finger under each word to help learners begin to recognize the words apart from the pictures.
4. Have the learners repeat the words at least three times.

> **I:** "Stove." (Point to the word.)
>
> **G:** "Stove."
>
> **I:** "Stove." (Underline the word with a finger. Motion for the group to repeat the word.)
>
> **G:** "Stove."

NOTE

Separating words from pictures should be done gradually and after plenty of practice.

5. Continue to review with the cards, using the previous pattern.
6. Fold cards in half to show only the words, to help learners become less dependent on the pictures.
7. Move from group to individual practice as learners become more comfortable reading the words without the assistance of the pictures.

Picture/Word Matching Activity

1. Shuffle the small picture and word cards together.
2. Distribute the cards to the learners, making sure that each learner has a card.
3. Have learners try to find pairs, matching a picture to a word.
4. Ask learners to stand up and mingle, identifying the noun card they hold (picture or word) to each person until they find their match, as in the example below.

> **Learner 1:** "Refrigerator." (Hold up the picture card.)
> **Learner 2:** "Refrigerator." (Hold up the word card.)

5. Have pairs sit down once they have made a correct match.
6. Put matched cards together and set them aside.
7. Reshuffle and redistribute the cards to the learners. Repeat the activity to help ensure all learners get practice reading the word cards.

Writing Activity

MATERIALS

Large vocabulary cards

Working/Not Working Checklist (one enlarged and one per learner)

Review

1. Shuffle all of the large noun cards together.
2. Show each card to the group while pronouncing each word slowly and clearly.
3. Run a finger under each word to help learners begin to recognize the words apart from the pictures.
4. Have the learners repeat the words at least three times.

> **I:** "Lock." (Point to the word.)
> **G:** "Lock."
> **I:** "Lock." (Underline the word with a finger. Motion for the group to repeat the word.)
> **G:** "Lock."

5. Continue to review with the cards, using the pattern above.

6. Fold cards in half to show only the words, to help learners become less dependent on the pictures.
7. Move from group to individual practice as learners become more comfortable reading the words without the assistance of the pictures.

Working/Not Working Checklist

1. Place an enlarged copy of the Working/Not Working Checklist in the front of the room.
2. Display the large vocabulary cards on the board, wall, or other available surface.
3. Distribute a Working/Not Working Checklist to each learner.
4. Ask learners to look at the pictures and decide if the items are working or not working.
5. Demonstrate how to look at the activity sheet and use the cards in the room to assist with completing each sentence.
6. On the enlarged copy of the activity sheet, model for learners how to write the appropriate words on the lines.
7. Have the learners complete the sentences on their own activity sheets with the appropriate nouns or adjectives.
8. Assist learners as necessary.

Renters' Responsibilities

VOCABULARY

NOUNS
Bill

House

Landlord (Owner)

Rent

Trash

NOUN PHRASES
Late fee

Loud music

VERBS
Call

Clean

Empty

Move

Pay

ADVERBS
Late

On time

Objective

Learners will understand that renters have certain responsibilities

Materials Included

- Storyboard
- Large reproducible vocabulary cards
- Small reproducible picture cards
- Good Renter activity board
- Circle the Correct Word activity sheet
- Storyboard Writing activity sheet
- **OK/Not OK** cards (page 250)

Materials Needed

- Additional instructor copy (enlarged) of the activity sheets
- A long piece of card stock or other instructor-devised method to use as a tapper (one per learner)
- Real or instructor-made replicas of paid bills and bills with due dates
- A calendar
- A radio or cassette player
- Real or play money
- Small objects to use as place markers (coins, buttons, paper clips, etc.)
- A die or coin

Civics Introduction

Renters' Responsibilities

It is important to know your responsibilities when entering into a rental agreement. Many rental agreements between a landlord and renter come in the form of a lease. A lease is a document that outlines expectations of both parties, such as location, rental period, monthly rent amount, and monthly payment date. Also, there is usually a security deposit required, which acts as insurance for the landlord if the renter should damage anything or break the lease agreement. A dated signature is needed from both parties to make the agreement legally binding. Once a lease is signed, any related written records, such as letters to the landlord and rent receipts, should be kept in a safe place.

Leases and rental agreements are legal documents, and by signing them, both parties are agreeing to abide by the terms. If a renter does not adhere to the agreement, he or she can be evicted after being served with legal papers. In most areas, these will give him or her 30 days notice to move, although there may be local variation. Any destruction of property resulting from the renter's negligence can result in the loss of the security deposit.

Leases also outline additional expenses, if any, that the renter must pay, as well as information about specific renter responsibilities. Some landlords might not pay for electricity, heat, or water. In other cases, landlords may pay for one or more of those basic utilities.

Whether or not there is a formal lease, renters have certain responsibilities, such as paying their rent on time. Trash disposal, general cleaning, and the proper operation of heating, plumbing, and electrical systems are also the renter's responsibilities. In areas where there is snow in the winter months, tenants may be expected to remove it from walkways or driveways, although in other cases, snow removal may be a landlord's responsibility. If a renter is living within close proximity to other apartments or houses, that renter is expected to maintain volume at acceptable levels on radios and televisions.

This topic is of special importance to newly arrived, non-English-speaking adults, as they frequently live in rental housing. They need to understand their responsibilities under a lease or rental agreement in order to fulfill their legal responsibilities and avoid any risk of eviction or forfeiting a security deposit. They also need to understand that renters are expected to maintain their dwellings by cleaning them and disposing of trash. Renters also need to report any maintenance problems with fixtures, such as plumbing, or utilities, such as heat.

Storyboard

MATERIALS

Storyboard

Introduce the Storyboard

1. Hold up each storyboard frame and point to each picture.
2. Ask the learners to identify items in the pictures.
3. Point to different parts of each frame to elicit known vocabulary.

> **I:** "What's this?" (Point to the house. Motion for the learners to respond.)

4. Narrate the storyboard using the following sentences:

> **Frame 1:** Pay rent on time.
> **Frame 2:** Clean the house.
> **Frame 3:** Empty trash.
> **Frame 4:** Call landlord.

5. Repeat the sentences that accompany the storyboard at least three times.

Oral Language Activity 1

Large noun cards (from Lessons A & B)

Storyboard frames

Small picture cards (two sets, each set on a different color of paper)

Real or instructor-made replicas of paid bills

Yes/No cards

Introduce the Target Nouns

1. Introduce the **house, rent,** and **landlord** cards by holding each card up for the group.
2. Point to items on the storyboard to reinforce the new terms.
3. Pronounce each word slowly and clearly and have the group repeat each word.

> **I:** "House." (Hold up the **house** card. Motion for the group to repeat together.)
> **G:** "House."
> **I:** "Good. House." (Motion for the group to repeat.)
> **G:** "House."
> **I:** "House." (Motion for the group to repeat. Put the **house** card at the front of the room.)
> **G:** "House."

4. Have the group repeat each new term at least three times.
5. Introduce the concept of ownership by picking up an object belonging to a learner.
6. Use learners' names and objects belonging to learners to model the possessive pattern.

> **I:** "José's pen." (Hold up a pen or other selected object and motion for the group to repeat.)
>
> **G:** "Jose's pen."
>
> **I:** "Maria's book." (Hold up a book or other selected object and motion for the group to repeat.)
>
> **G:** "Maria's book."

7. Repeat the pattern with various learners and their objects to teach the concept of ownership.
8. Use the **house** and **landlord** cards together to solidify the group's understanding of the concept that a landlord owns a rental property.

> **I:** "Landlord's house." (Hold up the **house** and **landlord** cards. Motion for the group to repeat.)
>
> **G:** "Landlord's house."

9. Review nouns from Lesson A by holding up each card and motioning for a response.
10. Assist learners as necessary.

NOTE

This can be a noncompetitive group activity or learners can remove the cards when they make a match. The learner with the most matched pairs wins.

Concentration Activity

1. Take the two sets of small picture cards, each on a different color of paper, and shuffle them together.
2. Set each card on the table facedown in rows and columns so that each card can be turned over easily.
3. Motion for the learners to watch and listen carefully by holding one hand up to an ear with palm open.
4. Turn over one card and identify it verbally.
5. Look for a corresponding card by turning over another card of a different color and identify it verbally.
6. Guide learners in how to carry out the activity by having an individual learner turn over cards and look for a match.
7. Model one success (learner keeps cards, takes another turn) and one failure (learner puts cards back, loses turn).

> **I:** "Ready?" (Motion for the learner to select a card and turn it over.)
>
> **I:** "What's this?" (Point to the card the learner has selected.)
>
> **L:** "House."
>
> **I:** "Good. Turn another card." (Motion for the learner to select another card and turn it over.)
>
> **I:** "What's this?" (Point to the card. Motion for the learner to identify it.)
>
> **L:** "House."
>
> **I:** "Match. OK." (Motion for the learner to keep the pair.)

8. Continue this activity by having the learner draw two more cards to find a match.
9. Have all of the learners take turns looking for pairs of cards and identifying each card verbally as it is turned over.
10. If the group has decided to collect pairs of cards, have each learner identify the pairs he or she holds at the end of the activity.
11. Repeat any of the words that learners have trouble remembering.

Comprehension Check

1. Collect the target noun cards and reshuffle them.
2. Introduce the cards one by one, identifying the nouns correctly and incorrectly at random.
3. Model how to say Yes when the card is correctly identified, and No when it is incorrectly identified.

> **I:** "Landlord" (Hold up the **landlord** card.)
>
> **I:** "Landlord. Yes." (Point to the **landlord** card and nod in agreement. Motion for the learners to repeat.)
>
> **G:** "Yes."
>
> **I:** "Bill." (Hold up the **landlord** card again.)
>
> **I:** "Bill. No." (Point to the **landlord** card and motion disagreement. Motion for the learners to repeat.)
>
> **G:** "No."

4. Continue with other target nouns at random, repeating words as necessary.

Oral Language Activity 2

MATERIALS

Large verb cards (two sets)

Large vocabulary cards

A long piece of card stock or other instructor-devised method to use as a tapper (one per learner and one for instructor)

Small picture cards (verbs only)

NOTE

Multiple sets of verb cards may be used for this activity. The activity can be done as a competition. In that case, the learner who collects the most cards wins.

Introduce the Target Verbs

1. Show each large verb card to the group while pronouncing each word slowly and clearly.

> **I:** "Pay." (Hold up the **pay** card. Motion for the group to repeat.)
>
> **G:** "Pay."
>
> **I:** "Good. Pay." (Motion for the group to repeat.)
>
> **G:** "Pay."
>
> **I:** "Pay." (Motion for the group to repeat. Put the **pay** card at the front of the room.)
>
> **G:** "Pay."

2. Introduce the target verbs using the format above.
3. Say each word and have the group repeat each one three times.
4. Repeat any words more than three times as necessary.

Tap Activity

1. Pass out tappers (one for each learner).
2. Set each small verb picture card down on the table faceup, without overlapping or crowding the cards, so that each picture can be seen clearly.
3. Motion for the learners to listen carefully by holding one hand up to an ear with palm open.
4. Hold up a large verb card and show it to the group, identifying it verbally.
5. Look for the corresponding small verb picture card and identify it with your tapper.
6. Motion for the learners to hold up their tappers to begin.

> **I:** "Ready?" (Hold up the tapper.)
>
> **G:** "OK."
>
> **I:** "Empty." (Hold up the verb card. Motion for the learners to try to quickly identify the corresponding small picture card and tap it.)

7. Ask the learner whose tapper identifies the correct card first to pick it up and say the word. Ask the group to repeat the term.

> **L:** "Pay." (Learner holds up the **pay** card.)

8. Repeat any of the verbs that learners have trouble remembering.

Comprehension Check

1. Shuffle the large vocabulary cards (nouns and verbs) and place them faceup on a table or other available surface.
2. Call out a target noun or verb and motion for the learners to try to pick up the corresponding card.
3. Have the learner who picks up the correct card first repeat the noun or verb. The learner should put the card back on the table.
4. Repeat this process until learners demonstrate comprehension of all of the target nouns and verbs.

Oral Language Activity 3

MATERIALS

Large noun, verb, and phrase cards (from Lessons A & B)

Multiple copies of the **not working** card (from Lesson A)

Bills with due dates

A calendar

OK/Not OK cards

Good Renter activity board

Place markers (one for each learner)

A die or coin

Real or play money

Introduce the Phrases and Adverbs

1. Introduce the phrases and adverbs by holding up each card, pronouncing each word slowly and clearly.
2. Use realia to clarify the meaning of the terms.

> **I:** "On time." (Hold up a calendar and a bill with a due date and compare the dates. Show the **on time** card.)
>
> **I:** "October 1st. Pay on October 1st. OK." (Point to the date on the bill and then the corresponding date on the calendar.)
>
> **I:** "On time." (Hold up the **on time** card and motion for the group to repeat.)
>
> **G:** "On time."
>
> **I:** "Good. On time." (Motion for the group to repeat.)
>
> **G:** "On time."
>
> **I:** "On time." (Motion for the group to repeat. Put the **on time** card at the front of the room.)
>
> **G:** "On time."

3. Repeat the dialogue above, using, for example, October 12th to teach the concept of **late.**

> **I:** "October 1st. Pay on October 12th. Not OK." (Point to the date on the bill and then the late date on the calendar. Hold up the **Not OK** card.)
>
> **I:** "Late." (Hold up the **late** card and motion for the group to repeat.)
>
> **G:** "Late."

4. Teach the concept of **late fee** using the calendar, a bill, and real or play money.
5. Hold up the calendar and point to the due date of the bill.

> **I:** "October 1st. Pay $400."
> **I:** "On time." (Point to October 1st.)
> **I:** "On time is OK." (Hold up the **OK** card. Gesture paying the amount on the bill {e.g., $400} on October 1st.)
> **I:** "Late." (Point to October 12th.)
> **I:** "Late is Not OK." (Hold up the **Not OK** card. Gesture paying $400 + $25.)
> **I:** "Late is Not OK."

6. Write the numbers used for the example on the board or on chart paper to help illustrate the concept of **late fee.**
7. Point to the $400. Using the calendar, show how a late fee (e.g., of $25) would be added to the bill if it was not on time (e.g., rent $400, fee $25, pay $425).

> **I:** "Fee. Late fee." (Point to the $25 amount. Motion for the group to repeat.)
> **G:** "Fee. Late fee."
> **I:** "Late fee." (Point to the $25 amount. Motion for the group to repeat.)
> **G:** "Late fee.
> **I:** "Late fee." (Point to the $25 amount. Motion for the group to repeat.)
> **G:** "Late fee."

8. Teach **loud music** by turning a radio or cassette player first to a normal volume.

> **I:** "OK." (Smile and mime enjoying the music.)

9. Turn the volume up high and cover your ears.

> **I:** "Not OK. Loud music. Not OK."
> **I:** "Loud music." (Hold up the **loud music** card. Motion for the group to repeat.)
> **G:** "Loud music."
> **I:** "Yes. Loud music." (Motion for the group to repeat.)
> **G:** "Loud music."
> **I:** "Loud music." (Motion for the group to repeat. Put the **loud music** card at the front of the room.)
> **G:** "Loud music."

10. Review the phrase **call landlord** from Lesson A and associate it with problems by holding up target nouns from Lesson A and the **not working** card.

> **I:** "What's this?" (Hold up the **stove** and **not working** cards.)
>
> **I:** "The stove is not working. Call landlord." (Point to the **stove** and **not working** cards.)
>
> **I:** "Call landlord." (Motion for the group to repeat.)
>
> **G:** "Call landlord."

11. Have the group repeat the verb phrase at least three times.
12. Have the group distinguish positive and negative behaviors by grouping cards identifying those behaviors in OK and Not OK columns.
13. Make two columns on the board or on chart paper. Put the **OK** and **Not OK** cards as headings of the two columns.
14. Ask learners where each card or combination of cards from Lessons A & B should be placed.

Examples

OK	Not OK
Clean house	Loud music
Empty trash	Stove not working
Call landlord	Electricity not working
Pay rent on time	Water not working

NOTE

The learner who completes the activity first is a good renter. When using a coin as a counter, heads = move two spaces and tails = move one space.

Good Renter Activity

1. Place the Good Renter activity board on a table or other surface that is accessible to learners.
2. Distribute a place marker to each learner (buttons, paper clips, coins, etc).
3. Have each learner take a turn by rolling a die or tossing a coin to move around the activity board.
4. Ask learners to identify the item or behavior pictured in the square where they land on the activity board.
5. Have learners who land on "good" behaviors advance two spaces.
6. Have learners who land on "bad" behaviors move back one space.
7. Assist the group as necessary.

Comprehension Check

1. Give each learner a set of **OK** and **Not OK** cards.
2. Use combinations of cards and hold up good and bad renter behaviors (one of each).

Example behaviors

Good behaviors	Bad behaviors
Pay/rent/on time	Pay/rent/late
Loud music/No	Loud music/Yes
Clean house/Yes	Clean house/No
Empty trash/Yes	Empty trash/No

3. Have the group associate each "good" behavior with the **OK** card. Have learners respond by saying *OK* and holding up the **OK** card when the cards for a good behavior are held up.
4. Have the group associate each "bad" behavior with the **Not OK** card. Have learners respond by saying *Not OK* and holding up the **Not OK** card when the cards for a bad behavior are held up.
5. Display all of the combinations of cards in a visible location.
6. Ask individual learners to identify one good renter behavior or one bad renter behavior.

Oral Language Activity 4

MATERIALS

Large vocabulary cards (multiple sets)

Introduce the Dialogue

1. Post the vocabulary cards on the board or on chart paper. Group cards to create the phrases used in the dialogue responses. Leave space to write the part of Speaker 2 next to or under the groupings.
2. Write the part of Speaker 1 on the board or on chart paper.
3. Point to yourself while reading the part of Speaker 1.
4. Write the part of Speaker 2 next to or under the vocabulary cards and point to the group while reading.

NOTE

Pointing to each word while reading is important to do even if the learners are non-readers or nonliterate.

Speaker 1:	"What do you do?" (Point to the **pay, rent,** and **on time** cards. Motion for a response.)
Speaker 2:	"Pay the rent on time."
Speaker 1:	"What do you do?" (Point to the **clean** and **house** cards. Motion for a response.)
Speaker 2:	"Clean the house."
Speaker 1:	"What do you do?" (Point to the **empty** and **trash** cards. Motion for a response.)
Speaker 2:	"Empty the trash."
Speaker 1:	"What do you do?" (Point to the **call** and **landlord** cards. Motion for a response.)
Speaker 2:	"Call the landlord."

5. Repeat the dialogue, with the instructor taking the role of Speaker 1 and the group taking the role of Speaker 2.

Dialogue Activity

1. Write the sample dialogue (see example below) on the board or on chart paper.
2. Place groupings of vocabulary cards for each response in the dialogue in order from left to right on the board or in another visible location.
3. Point to each card while saying the dialogue. Ask the target question and have learners respond, based on the identified cards.
4. As necessary, model a response and have learners repeat if they cannot respond on their own.

Speaker 1: "What do you do?" (Point to the **pay, rent,** and **on time** cards. Motion for a response.)
Speaker 2: "Pay the rent on time."
Speaker 1: "What do you do?" (Point to the **clean** and **house** cards. Motion for a response.)
Speaker 2: "Clean the house."
Speaker 1: "What do you do?" (Point to the **empty** and **trash** cards. Motion for a response.)
Speaker 2: "Empty the trash."
Speaker 1: "What do you do?" (Point to the **call** and **landlord** cards. Motion for a response.)
Speaker 2: "Call the landlord."

5. Perform the dialogue by using the cards and taking the role of Speaker 1. Have the group respond to the instructor as Speaker 2.
6. Run a finger under each sentence whenever the dialogue is repeated in this activity.

Comprehension Check

1. Ask the target question from the dialogue and hold up vocabulary cards to prompt a response.

I: "What do you do?" (Hold up the **pay, rent,** and **on time** cards. Motion for learners to respond.)
G: "Pay the rent on time."

2. Distribute sets of cards that illustrate the responses in the dialogue above to learners.

3. Ask learners each question from the dialogue. Prompt learners' response to each question and ask learners to hold up the corresponding set of cards as they respond.

> **I:** "What do you do?" (Hold up the **clean** and **house** cards. Motion for learners to respond.)
>
> **L:** "Clean the house." (Learner should hold up the **clean** and **house** cards.)

4. Complete the Comprehension Check by asking all of the dialogue questions and having learners respond appropriately by holding up the corresponding cards.

Reading Activity

MATERIALS

Large noun cards (from Lessons A & B)

Circle the Correct Word activity sheet (one enlarged and one per learner)

Review

1. Shuffle all of the target noun cards.
2. Show each card to the group while pronouncing each word slowly and clearly.
3. Run a finger under each word to help learners begin to recognize the words apart from the pictures.
4. Have the learners repeat the words at least three times.

> **I:** "Bill." (Point to the word.)
>
> **G:** "Bill."
>
> **I:** "Bill." (Underline the word with a finger. Motion for the group to repeat the word.)
>
> **G:** "Bill."

NOTE

Separating words from pictures should be done gradually and after plenty of practice.

5. Continue to review with the cards, using the pattern above.
6. Fold cards in half to show only the words, to help learners become less dependent on the pictures.
7. Move from group to individual practice as learners become more comfortable reading the words without the assistance of the pictures.

Circle the Correct Word Activity Sheet

1. Distribute a Circle the Correct Word activity sheet to each learner.
2. Post the enlarged copy of the activity sheet at the front of the room or in another visible location.
3. Place a set of vocabulary cards in a visible location.
4. Provide an example of completing the activity by modeling with the enlarged activity sheet.

5. Point to the pictures and words on the activity sheet.
6. Ask the group to identify the first picture.
7. Guide the group in looking at the word choices and identifying the correct term corresponding to the picture.
8. Have learners refer to the posted vocabulary cards for assistance.
9. Demonstrate how to circle the correct term.

> **I:** "What's this?" (Point to the picture of the house. Motion for the learners to respond.)
>
> **G:** "House."
>
> **I:** "Good. Where's *house?*" (Point to the word choices. Ask the learners to look at the displayed cards and find the corresponding word. Gesture looking at the choices to find the word *house.*)
>
> **I:** "Here it is. House." (Circle the corresponding word.)

10. Complete the activity sheet as a group.

Writing Activity

MATERIALS

Large noun cards (from Lessons A & B)

Storyboard Writing activity sheet (one enlarged and one per learner)

Review

1. Shuffle all of the target noun cards together.
2. Show each card to the group while pronouncing each word slowly and clearly.
3. Run a finger under each word to help learners begin to recognize the words apart from the pictures.
4. Have the learners repeat the words at least three times.

> **I:** "Bill." (Point to the word.)
>
> **G:** "Bill."
>
> **I:** "Bill." (Underline the word with a finger. Motion for the group to repeat the word.)
>
> **G:** "Bill."

NOTE

Separating words from pictures should be done gradually and after plenty of practice.

5. Continue to review with the cards, using the pattern above.
6. Fold cards in half to show only the words, to help learners become less dependent on the pictures.
7. Move from group to individual practice as learners become more comfortable reading the words without the assistance of the pictures.

Storyboard Writing Activity Sheet

1. Post an enlarged copy of the activity sheet in the front of the room or other visible location.
2. Review with the group each set of vocabulary cards that correspond to the sentences for the storyboard frames.

Storyboard Frames

Frame 1: Pay rent on time.
Frame 2: Clean the house.
Frame 3: Empty trash.
Frame 4: Call landlord.

3. Point to each frame and say the corresponding sentence.

> **I:** "Pay rent on time." (Hold up the **pay, rent,** and **on time** cards.)

4. Demonstrate the activity on the enlarged activity sheet by writing each word one at a time in the spaces provided.
5. Read the phrase again, pointing to each word while reading.
6. Ask the learners to write the phrase for the first frame in the correct spaces on their activity sheets.
7. Show learners each phrase by writing each one on the board or in another visible location before completing the activity sheet.
8. Have the group write each phrase in the correct place to label each frame on their own activity sheets.

5 Unit Review Activity

MATERIALS

Unit Review Activity Sheet (one enlarged and one per learner)

Large vocabulary cards (from Lessons A & B)

NOTE

The Unit Review Activity can be done as a group activity for reinforcing the concepts learned in the lesson or done as an individual activity for assessment purposes.

Good or Bad Renter Review Activity

1. Use large vocabulary cards from Lessons A and B to review the vocabulary and concepts of the unit.
2. Post an enlarged copy of the activity sheet in the front of the room or in another visible location.
3. Point to each picture on the enlarged activity sheet and ask learners to identify it. Help learners combine the sets of pictures (in items 1, 2, 3, and 6) to create complex actions or sentences (e.g., in item 3, students could say *Pay rent late*).
4. Distribute a copy of the Unit Review Activity sheet to each learner.
5. On the enlarged activity sheet, point to the picture or set of pictures in each item. Elicit from learners whether the action or combination in the item is an appropriate action (a good renter behavior) or an inappropriate behavior (a bad renter behavior).
6. Model how learners should circle Yes for good behaviors and No for bad behaviors.
7. Ask learners to complete the activity on their own sheets.
8. Assist learners as necessary.

Central Theme Picture

Gas

✂

Electricity

Heater

Lock

Sink

Refrigerator

Shower

Stove

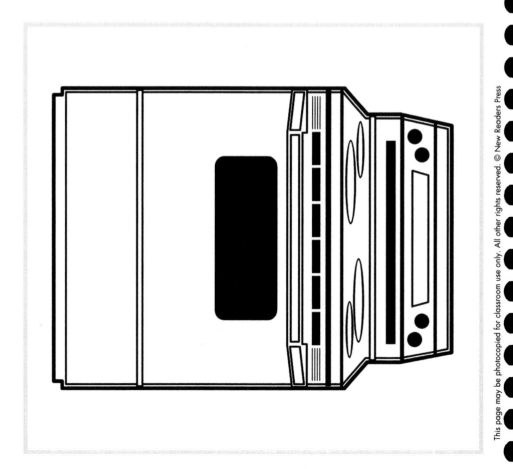

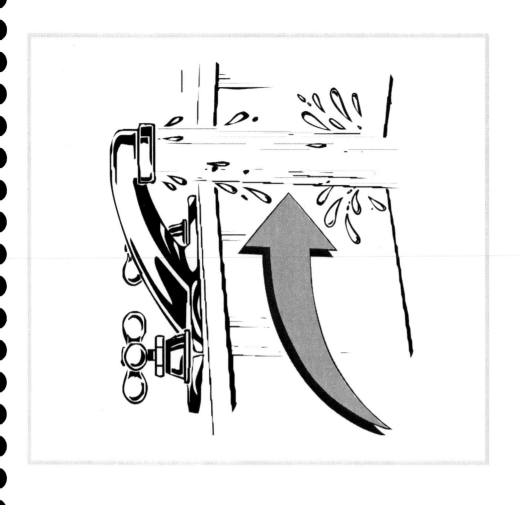

Water

Unit 5 Maintaining Housing Lesson A Life Skill

✂

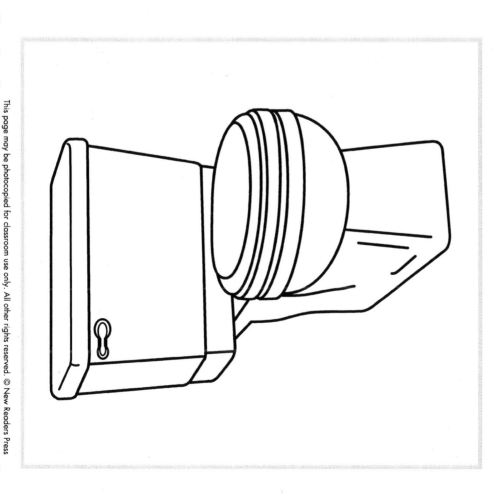

Toilet

Unit 5 Maintaining Housing Lesson A Life Skill

Window

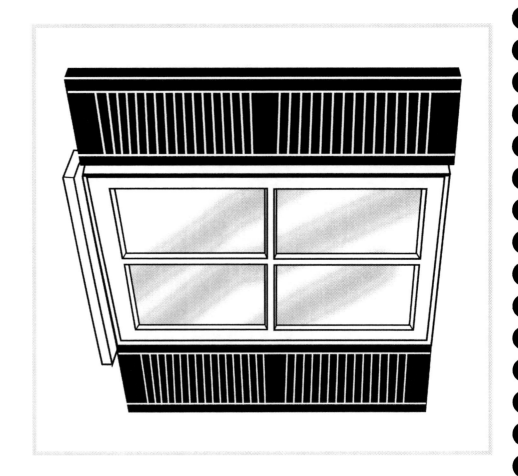

✂

No

Yes

Not Working

Unit 5 *Maintaining Housing* Lesson A *Life Skill*

Working

Unit 5 *Maintaining Housing* Lesson A *Life Skill*

Unit 5 *Maintaining Housing* Lesson A   Small Picture Cards

Unit 5 *Maintaining Housing* Lesson A   Small Picture Cards

Unit 5 *Maintaining Housing* Lesson A   Small Picture Cards

Unit 5 *Maintaining Housing* Lesson A   Small Picture Cards

Unit 5 *Maintaining Housing* Lesson A   Small Picture Cards

Unit 5 *Maintaining Housing* Lesson A   Small Picture Cards

Unit 5 *Maintaining Housing* Lesson A   Small Picture Cards

Unit 5 *Maintaining Housing* Lesson A   Small Picture Cards

Unit 5 *Maintaining Housing* Lesson A   Small Picture Cards

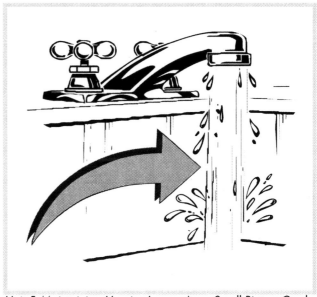

Unit 5 *Maintaining Housing* Lesson A   Small Picture Cards

Unit 5 *Maintaining Housing* Lesson A   Small Picture Cards

Unit 5 *Maintaining Housing* Lesson A   Small Picture Cards

Unit 5 *Maintaining Housing* Lesson A   Small Picture Cards

Unit 5 *Maintaining Housing* Lesson A   Small Picture Cards

Working

Unit 5 *Maintaining Housing* Lesson A   Small Word Cards

Not Working

Unit 5 *Maintaining Housing* Lesson A   Small Word Cards

Electricity

Gas

Heater

Lock

Refrigerator

Sink

Shower

Stove

Toilet

Water

Window

Mini Picture Bingo Board 1

Unit 5 Lesson A   Mini Picture Bingo Boards

Mini Picture Bingo Board 2

Unit 5 Lesson A   Mini Picture Bingo Boards

Mini Picture Bingo Board 3

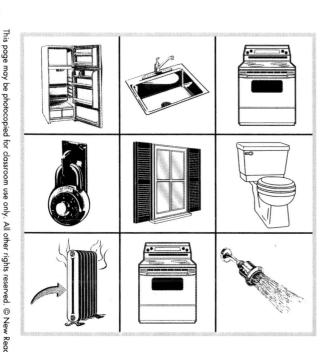

Unit 5 Lesson A   Mini Picture Bingo Boards

Mini Picture Bingo Board 4

Unit 5 Lesson A   Mini Picture Bingo Boards

Working/Not Working Checklist

Look at the pictures. Write the words. Check Working or Not Working.

Working **Not working**

1. No

<u>No</u>　　<u>gas</u>　　<u>heater</u>　　　　✔

2. No

3. Yes

4. Yes

5. No

Unit 5 *Maintaining Housing* Lesson A *Life Skill*

Writing Activity Sheet

Unit 5 Lesson B   Storyboard Frame 1

Unit 5 Lesson B   Storyboard Frame 2

Unit 5 Lesson B   Storyboard Frame 3

Unit 5 Lesson B   Storyboard Frame 4

Bill

✂

House

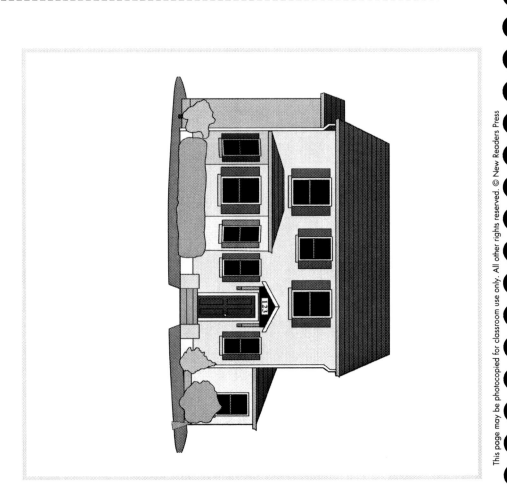

Rent

Landlord
(owner)

Trash

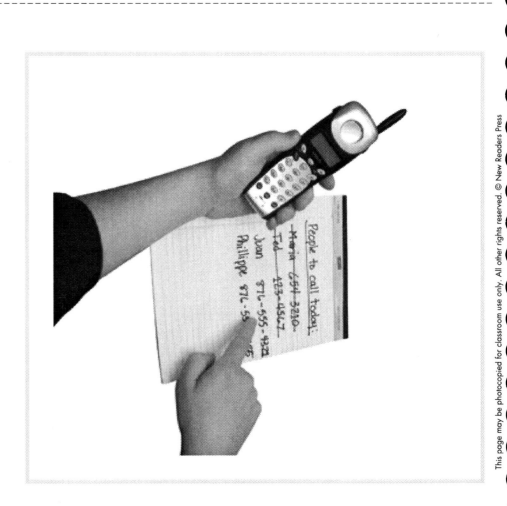

✂ -

Call

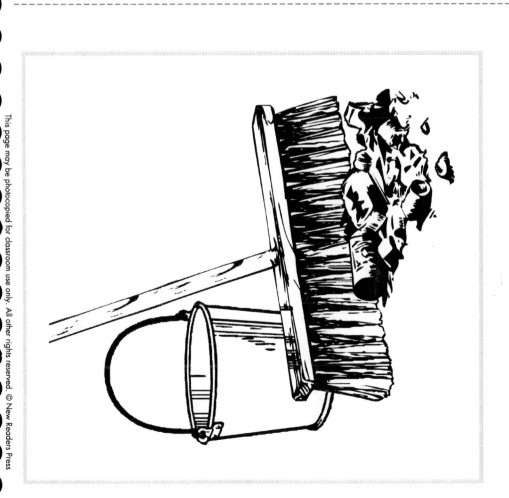

Empty

Clean

Move

Pay

Late fee

Late

Loud music

On time

Unit 5 Lesson B   Small Picture Cards

Unit 5 Lesson B   Small Picture Cards

Unit 5 Lesson B   Small Picture Cards

Unit 5 Lesson B   Small Picture Cards

Unit 5 Lesson B   Small Picture Cards

Unit 5 Lesson B   Small Picture Cards

Unit 5 Lesson B   Small Picture Cards

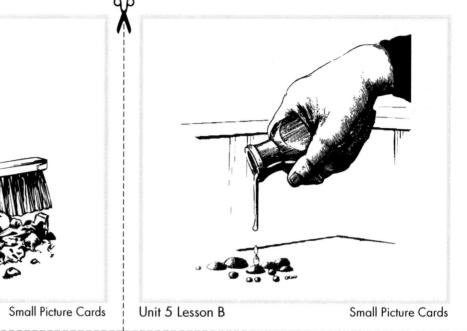

Unit 5 Lesson B   Small Picture Cards

Unit 5 Lesson B   Small Picture Cards

Unit 5 Lesson B   Small Picture Cards

Unit 5 Lesson B   Small Picture Cards

Unit 5 Lesson B   Small Picture Cards

244

Unit 5 Lesson B   Small Picture Cards

Unit 5 Lesson B   Small Picture Cards

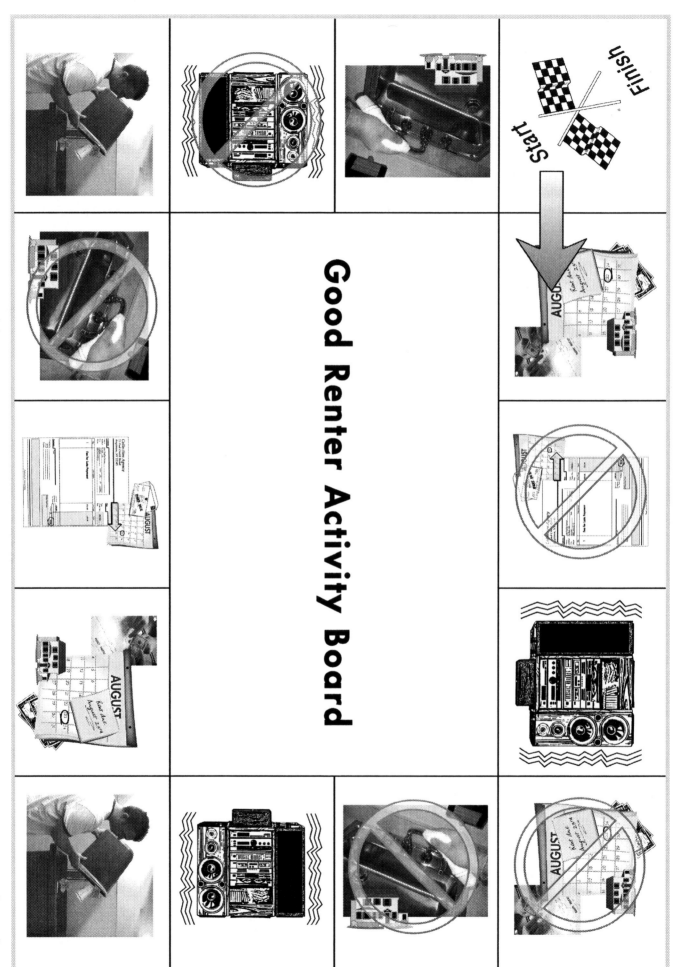

Good Renter Activity Board

Start
Finish

Circle the Correct Word Activity

Look at the pictures. Circle the correct word.

1.	Call	House	Trash
2.	Landlord	Rent	On time
3.	Pay	Bill	Rent
4.	Trash	Late	Landlord
5.	House	Bill	Empty
6.	Rent	Call	Move

Unit 5 Maintaining Housing Lesson B *Civic Responsibility*

Reading Activity Sheet

Storyboard Writing Activity

Look at each storyboard frame. Write the correct phrase on the lines.

1.

_____ _____ _____ _____ .

2.

_____ _____ _____ .

3.

_____ _____ .

4.

_____ _____ .

Look at each group of pictures. Circle Yes or No for each group.

1.     Yes   No

2.  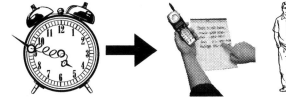   Yes   No

3.   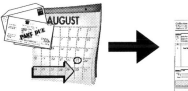    Yes   No

4.   Yes   No

5.    Yes   No

6.      Yes   No

OK

Not OK